John B. Morrall.

THE TRUEST TRAGEDY
A Study of Plato's Laws

Angelos Kargas

MINERVA PRESS
LONDON
ATLANTA MONTREUX SYDNEY

THE TRUEST TRAGEDY: *A Study of Plato's Laws*
Copyright © Angelos Kargas 1998

All Rights Reserved

No part of this book may be reproduced in any form
by photocopying or by any electronic or mechanical means,
including information storage or retrieval systems,
without permission in writing from both the copyright
owner and the publisher of this book.

ISBN 0 75410 435 4

First Published 1998 by
MINERVA PRESS
195 Knightsbridge
London SW7 1RE

Printed in Great Britain for Minerva Press

THE TRUEST TRAGEDY
A Study of Plato's Laws

This book is dedicated to Eleni...

Voices ideal and beloved
of those who have died, or of those
who are lost for us like the dead.

Sometimes in dreams they speak to us;
sometimes within thinking the brain hears them.

And with the sound of them for a moment return
sounds from the first poetry of our life –
like music, at night, in the distance, that dies away.

'Voices' by Constantine P. Cavafy

Acknowledgements

A very special thanks to my parents Vasiliki and Yiannis Kargas for the immeasurable gifts of my life, above all their ongoing faith in me, their patience, and their efforts to help me see the light at the end of every tunnel.

My gratitude goes also to Dr Anne Sheppard, from whose thought and humanity I have profited in too many ways to mention, for her enthusiastic encouragement, availability and significant contribution to the publication of this book.

July 1998

Preface

The topic of my research is Plato's *Laws*. In my first chapter I describe the *Laws* as a new kind of drama, considering Plato's own description of the work as the 'truest tragedy'. My main argument concerning the *Laws* as drama is based on the following four assumptions: first, in the use of the dialogue form; second, as in a true religious drama, there is the divine background; third, it covers similar themes to those of tragedy; fourth, a number of themes are woven together so that there is an 'interplay' of themes comparable with the interplay of characters, if not necessarily of themes, in a play.

The *Laws* is a tragedy that has proper *paideia* in its heart, intending to teach the individual the way to use his reason properly. Yet was designed to influence and challenge the way the Greeks understood the relation between drama and philosophy. If tragedy is to fulfil its goals, must be placed within the philosophical context of reasoning. Hence, the *Laws* is a true tragedy in Plato's required sense of tragedy, as the arousal of emotion is now replaced by stimulating reason. It is a tragedy that represents what is truly serious and shows how to acquire the fine and noble life. This is in contrast to the Greek tragedies which on the whole provided the wrong models of life for Plato, due to their emotional effects which fed the baser part of men's souls.

My second chapter is concerned with the organisation of the state, and is mostly about how Magnesia would be organised and governed. I have included discussions on the themes of women, homosexuality, marriage, freedom and education, and have drawn contrasts and parallels with other Platonic works in order to state that when one discusses Plato's political philosophy one should not identity him as a totalitarian because of his idealistic and utopian ideas of the *Republic*. Indeed, in the *Laws*, Plato states that the best form of government is a combination of both democracy and monarchy, a form of government that many European countries enjoy today.

This chapter intends to emphasise that the majority of Plato's views in the *Laws* are on the whole consistent with those expressed in his other works. Moreover it intends to stress that one should not be concerned with the inconsistencies in Plato's state, but with whether Plato fulfils his proposed aim and offers a workable plan to be adopted by a new city in his time.

In my third chapter I consider the crucial religious aspects of the *Laws*. I aim to show how Plato conceived the relation between man and God or Gods, and with the validity of his demonstration of divine existence. I conclude that the *Laws* represent the beginning of a new age, and that for Plato the cause of the laws of any state is a perfectly rational process. The *Laws* also justifies that the role of philosophy is still important in the governing of the new state where the condemnation of sophistry and ancient mythology is essential.

In my fourth chapter I portray the *Laws* as the first work in the ancient literature of jurisprudence, as Plato for the first time draws an explicit theoretical distinction between private and public courts. Plato now understands why the rule of law requires the provision of an executive of magistrates, a system of courts and a body of members of the judiciary. He understands that the court is an agent of coercion and repression and should also have the related task of re-education. Above all he shows that the *entelecheia* (entelechy) of Magnesia is nothing else but the law itself.

Contents

Introduction		xi
I	A Preface to the *Laws*	21
	Plato's Criticism on Poetry	24
	On Reading a Platonic Dialogue	29
	The *Laws* as a New Kind of Drama	33
II	The Organisation of the State	48
	The Place of Magnesia in Plato's Thought	48
	The Material Assumptions for the Establishment of Magnesia	50
	The Magnesian Social Classes and the Continuation of Plato's Social Philosophy	52
	Paideia in Magnesia	55
	The Individual and his Freedom	61
	Women in Classical Attic and their Images in Literature	67
	Equality of Education as a Sufficient Factor in the Equality of the Sexes	71
	Women in the *Laws*	75
	Male Homosexuality	78
	Female Homosexuality	86
III	Gods, Heroes and the Theocracy of *Laws* IV	90
	The Philosophical Theology of *Laws* X	104
	The Good Man in the *Laws*: His Attitude to Pleasure and Honour	114
	Plato and Philosophy	119

IV		127
	Introduction	127
	Dike, Dikaion and Dikaiosyne from Homer to the Sophists 'The Old Stories Contain Elements of Truth'	132
	(a) Homer and Hesiod	132
	(b) Nature and Convention: the Presocratics and the Sophists	136
	Plato's Response: the Necessity for Justice, Jurisprudence and Medical Punishment	142
Epilogue		162
Bibliography		166
Classical Texts and Translations		173
List of Periodicals		176

Introduction

In a state of intellectual excitement straight after completing the thesis for my MA on Plato's *Republic*, I read the *Laws* closely and with growing fascination, allowing myself to be absorbed by it. Thus, in writing about the *Laws*, my choice of this work is not arbitrary. It is a reflection of my internal need for consciousness and my philosophical thirst for a better acquaintance with it. In short, it is an act of pure love for the work and an opportunity to allow myself to express my conviction that the system of the dialogue has many ramifications.

When making any enquiry into the *Laws*, one hardly knows where to begin the discussion. More importantly, it is difficult to know where to terminate it, if parallels on particular issues have to be drawn between the *Laws* and other earlier Platonic works. My research was of some necessity to me for two main reasons.

First, the *Laws*[1] has been neglected since ancient times; throughout the rise of Christianity, and indeed up until the nineteenth century, there have been hardly any comments or literature on the dialogue. Plato has been mainly identified with the doctrines of the *Republic* and a few closely connected dialogues.[2] Even some of those who have argued for the authenticity of the *Laws* and have neglected the tradition that it was written either in whole or in part by Philip of Opus[3] (who is said to have copied it out of Plato's notes) have

---

[1] Planinc, 1991, p.155. Post, 1934.

[2] Some discussions worthy of attention concerned with the recent history of interpretation of the Laws may be found in the following works: Guthrie, 1978, pp.321–323; Morrow, 1960, pp.515–18; Saunders, 1979; Stalley, 1983, pp.1 ff.; Jaeger, 1943, III, p.213.

[3] Formally, one of these, the *Epinomis*, is an appendix to the *Laws*, of which it was occasionally called the thirteenth book, because it answers the question of how to attain the highest state of virtue and bliss demanded of members of the Nocturnal Council in the *Laws*, Book XII. However, the authenticity of the Epinomis has been doubted over the centuries on the basis of its content and of it style.

From Zeller (1876) onwards the general objection has been that the wisdom required there of the members of the Nocturnal Council is not that of Platonism but rather a kind of theosophy.

nevertheless felt it does not contain material worthy of study and so have often excluded the *Laws* from discussion.

Second, in spite of the fact that there have been recent studies of the *Laws*, the majority of them explicitly regard it as being of little literary value and portray it as the least attractive and least prestigious work of philosophical literature in the Platonic corpus, whereas I intend to argue the contrary.

A great number of scholars have been concerned either with the *Laws'* internal inconsistencies, contradictions and apparently rambling sentences, or its continuity and discontinuity with the *Republic*. In this way they suggest Plato's diminished capacity to write as a philosophical dramatist and claim to show the limitations of the literary standard of the work.

Yet I am fully aware also of a number of valuable interpretations and analyses of the dialogue by scholars like Leo Strauss, Eric Voegelin and Thomas Pangle, who have felt it necessary to recover something of the Aristotelian comment on the *Laws* and Aristotle's description of it as a work that is 'witty, original, and searching', that is, 'beyond measure'.[4] They have felt it is one-sided to focus exclusively on the *Republic* when discussing Plato's ethico-political philosophy, since the *Laws*, like the *Republic*, contains material worthy of speculation and consideration, material written by a great philosophical dramatist that ought to be approached and taken seriously both philosophically and dramatically.

The *Laws* is a work in which Plato does not pose the question of definition, 'What is law?' as he did in what are now called 'first period' or 'elenctic' dialogues, but rather indirectly a modal question 'How is law?' Where is the importance of this Law to be found? What is its purpose and role? It was the modalities of law and its relationship with social change that occupied the core of Plato's thinking when he wrote the *Laws*. It is also a work in which Plato

---

Müller, who in 1951 argued for a view of the *Laws* as a chaotic product of Plato's decline, amongst other German scholars has also argued against Taylor that the author of the *Epinomis* was not Plato. Taylor on the other hand has argued that the *Epinomis* was regularly quoted as Plato's from Cicero onwards and that we do not know the actual name of any writer before Proclus who doubted its authenticity.

The common ascription of the *Epinomis* to the astronomer Philip of Opus must rest wholly on external evidence, since no work of his has survived. We have the statement of Diogenes Laertius: 'Some say that Philip of Opus transcribed Plato's *Laws* from the wax tablets. They also say that the *Epinomis* is Philip's' (DL III 37). I believe that there cannot be a definite verdict as to the authenticity of the *Epinomis* and so any scholar, like Zeller, Jaeger and Wilamowitz, should avoid stating dogmatically that the work is Philip's as the evidence we have is not sufficient to provide an argument for or against its authenticity.

See also Stalley, 1983, pp.2–3.

[4] Aristole, *Politics*, 1265a, 12–14.

describes how what we now term deliberate, legislative, executive and judicial bodies should operate, and how political power in general should be exercised. The *Laws* is thus more than a mere description and exposition of the institutions and laws that would be appropriate for the new city to be established.

At the same time it is a work that shows Plato's knowledge of current Greek law and institutions which he was reshaping in order to offer the best conditions for a practicable plan for fourth century states and statesmen, perhaps to be implemented in Sicily after the death of Dionysius, when the restoration of the Sicilian towns was necessary.[5]

Thus, Plato, some thirty years after his composition of the *Republic*, is not merely concerned with theory but with putting the latter into practice.[6] As the eminent scholar Glen Morrow has masterfully showed in his book *Plato's Cretan City*, Plato obviously had a good awareness and comprehensive knowledge of the traditions, laws and political institutions in force in Sparta, Crete and Athens.[7] He nevertheless felt the wrongfulness of some of the laws and institutions in all three states, and considered it his task to respond to the needs of a craftsman legislator who was about to found Magnesia.

Those who have appreciated Plato's intention in the work have indeed contributed their own understanding of it and have ignored controversies about Plato's technique in the *Laws*. They instead have been concerned with his treatment of fundamental questions of political and legal philosophy. However, in spite of the fact that they have evidently appreciated the importance of the *Laws* as containing Plato's final thoughts on the significance and method of education, the secret of a stable constitution, a theory of punishment and penology, a discussion of individual responsibility, and an elaborate proof of the existence of God or Gods whilst helping man to conceive his relation to God, I feel that in their research they have been prisoners of their existing conceptions of what are the most important aspects of the work. Consequently, they have followed and taken up what they suppose to be important while they have left out of their discussions what they consider less important, or have paid very little attention to it.

I therefore, have decided to attempt to further their valuable knowledge and understanding of the work, in adding my own. However, even though I am fully aware of and appreciate the works of Strauss, Pangle, Voegelin,

---

[5] Morrow, 1960, p.7.

[6] Ibid., 1960, p.4; Plato, *Politicus*, 260 a–b. Plato states that the scientific statesman cannot be content with theoretical principles alone but must supplement them with directions for action. See also *Phil*, 62 a–b.

[7] Morrow, 1960, p.6. See also Rostovtzeff, 1929, pp.1, 337–8.

Morrow, Saunders and Taylor amongst many others and will take account of what they have actually said, I will not engage in polemical controversy with their arguments for and against the *Laws* except incidentally. Nor shall I be concerned to mount an attack on scholars who, when generalising about Plato or about the history of political thought, have either discussed the *Laws* only briefly or left it out of their accounts altogether.[8]

I understand that all interpretative essays on the *Laws*, however apparently broad the vista they presume to afford, remain partial views. My own assertion of the significant aspects of the dialogue may allow some to say that I too am a prisoner of my own conception, individual impression and evaluation of this work. However, this is simply because 'to describe', as A.W. Gouldner has written, 'is to select, to select is to evaluate; to evaluate is to criticise'.[9] To criticise, I might add, is already to construct. Criticism implies a point of view, a standard of fact. My enterprise may be found to contain some errors, but I hope that their correction by others will lead to further investigation of problems partially exposed and no doubt imperfectly solved here, so that there may be increasing attention paid to the *Laws*.

As for the plan I shall adopt here, it is true that I do not have one main topic preceded by certain preliminary enquiries and followed by others. My plan may therefore seem somewhat arbitrary, especially if we consider the traditional way of treating a Platonic dialogue in modern scholarship where there is normally some sort of plan based on a central topic. However, I would view this as inaccurate, since works of literary criticism about the investigation of Platonic dialogues carry titles which do not in fact reflect the whole content of the work but only part of them.

More importantly, if I desire to guarantee my fidelity to the *Laws*, and consequently establish a firm and enduring interpretation of them, I must preserve what Plato himself was doing in this work, that, as expressed in my opening paragraph, has many ramifications and not only one topic.

The Laws divides into two parts: (a) the introductory part comprising of the first three books, which I take as a preamble to the main part that follows, and (b) the main, or legislative part, extending from Book IV to the end of the work.

Of the first three introductory books, only the third is intimately connected with what follows, and comprises a special part concerned with the origins,

---

[8] Barker, 1960, pp.14, 207–8, 226–7, especially when generalising about Plato or about the history of Greek political thought. Yet I am aware that in his book *The Political Thought of Plato and Aristotle* he discusses the *Laws* briefly.
[9] Gouldner, 1965, p.168.

development, preservation and destruction of cities. The first two examine the beginning and concept of legislation stating what its purpose should be, and specifying the ethical conditions for the establishment of a state as well as the educational means that contribute to its ethical basis.

At first sight it seems curious and rather inexplicable that the greatest part of Book I and the whole of Book II[10] is a *logos peri oinou*, that is, a discussion about wine and drinking as Plato explicitly states it.[11] The subject matters of the rather long *logos peri oinou* are the *symposia*, the excess of drink, and the educational meaning of the drinking parties. The last subject of Plato's discussion on *oinologia* (drinking) is the most important one, as it also appears from the statement of Kleinias.[12] In addition to that, the long discussion *peri methés* (about drunkenness) surrounds the discussion *peri choreias* (about the chorus) of Book II. This is the reason why many interpreters take the latter discussion to be the main subject of Book II.

In both books the *logos peri oinou* concerns the problem of *paideia* and the need to define the latter.[13] Moreover, Plato himself states how this is related to his discussions of *peri mousikés* (about music) and *peri paideias* (about education) in particular.[14]

The second part of the *Laws* starts with Book IV. The latter[15] is mostly concerned with *oroi*, the conditions for the establishment of the new city: geographical position, the origin of the colonists, the possible development of life in the state. It is worth noting that during the establishment of the state, Plato neither attributes a name to the new state nor states the exact position. It is only in Book VII[16] that the citizens of the new state are called Magnétes (Magnesians). Thus we tend to think that the name of the city would be Magnesia.

Plato's reluctance to state the name of the city makes it apparent that the city created in this work was neither meant to prove relevant only to one legislative need, nor to be used only for one particular state. It was not based on a particular geographical reality; it was a creature of a philosophical intention. Straight after the statements concerned with the geographical and anthropological conditions for the establishment of Magnesia, Plato starts the

---

[10] Plato, *Laws*, I 637a–II 674c.
[11] Ibid., II 674c.
[12] Ibid., I 641c.
[13] Ibid., I 643.
[14] Ibid., I 642b.
[15] Ibid., IV 715e.
[16] Ibid., VII 848d.

legislative part of the work whilst stating the great *genikon prooimion* (general preamble) of the whole legislation.[17] I take this preamble as a kind of a general introductory statement of the whole legislation in the *Laws*. However, in addition to this preamble, Plato puts other preambles before a proposed law.[18]

The legislative part of the work starts from Book V.[19] Indeed, until the end of Book V, Plato constructs in a legislative way everything concerning the establishment of the colonists' *katoikismos* (settlement) (the number of the citizens, the division of the citizens into classes, the division of the land and the households).

In Book VI of the *Laws*, presents all the legislation concerning the rulers of the state.[20] From Book VI[21] until the end of the dialogue are given laws according to the phases of human life, and in Book VI Plato details the laws concerning marriage, birth, the treatment of slaves. The whole of Book VII is concerned with the upbringing and the education of the young.[22]

Book VIII regulates in a legislative way the purpose of *paideia* in the adult life of men, and is concerned with the military obligations of the young in the common *symposia*, the relations between the two sexes, financial life and the productive class.

In the last four books that follow we have an exposition of penal provisions. Book IX is concerned with capital offences; Book X deals with offences against the Gods and thus tackles religion and theology. Book XI is concerned with family laws and Book XII with offences against the state. The last part of the latter[23] is concerned with the *orthon syllogon* (Nocturnal Council), that is responsible for the enforcement of law and order so that the new state will be preserved.

In order to achieve my aim, I shall be following a rather Aristotelian approach in that I shall be starting with what is known.

> We must start what is known. But things are known in two senses: known to us and known absolutely. Presumably we must start from what is known to us. So if anyone wants to make a serious study of ethics (fine and just things) or of political science generally, he must

---

[17] Plato, *Laws*, IV 715e–v 734e.
[18] Ibid., 729b, 730c–731b, 903b.
[19] Ibid., V 735a.
[20] Ibid., VI 751a–771a.
[21] Ibid., VI 771a.
[22] Ibid., VI 771a–775b.
[23] Ibid., 960e.

have been well trained in his habits, for the starting point is the fact, and if this is sufficiently clear there will be no need to ascertain the reason why.[24]

I shall be starting my research on the *Laws* from what is known to me, from the dialogue itself and from historians, orators and philosophers of the same period as the writing of the *Laws*, as well as what has become known to me from modern scholars.

First in my exposition of the dialogue is Plato's relation to, and attack on, Greek poetic tradition, since logically the interpreter ought to engage first with Plato's means of expression. He must offer some account of Plato's most original and characteristic tendencies, the dialogue form in particular and show whether Plato still maintains the dramatic form and content of his earlier dialogues. In short, I conclude that although the *Laws* may not be the most artfully dramatic work of Platonic philosophy, there might be an explanation for this. I presume it is because Plato aims to come down to the level of everyday reality, in any case, it is, in its own way, as dramatic as other Platonic works. To put it in the Athenian's words, 'It is the truest tragedy'.[25]

Hence my first chapter will describe the *Laws* as drama, considering the Athenian's own words more than those of modern commentators. I shall offer an appraisal of the *Laws'* dramatic context, including comments on all three characters that participate in the setting of the dialogue. Each of these can be seen as a reflection of the drama of the city he represents. This appraisal of the dramatic context of the characters and the setting of the dialogue, as presented in the first three books of the work, shows us that Plato intended them to be some sort of introduction to the rest of the work. From Book IV onwards, Plato describes in immense detail the requirements for the system of law and government for the new city. Following this book, the drama of the dialogue increases. This is because the subject of the *Laws* is no longer, as in the *Republic*, the ideal city to be ruled by philosophers nor, as in *Politicus*, a man who should possess the 'science of kingship'. Plato's object now is to search for the best possible laws to give birth to a new state and consequently offer living unity and harmonisation. This is not to say that in the *Republic* he is unconcerned with the above issues; he is, but in a different way, as his interests lay elsewhere. In the *Republic* he is concerned with a utopian plan, whereas in the *Laws* he no longer expects the city to live according to the

---

[24] Aristotle, *Nicomachean Ethics*, 1095b, 2–10.
[25] Plato, *Laws*, 817b–c.

directives of the form of the good; instead, he sets up precise rules for education in order to make citizens as enlightened as possible, and imposes punishments to head off any threat of corruption before it is too late.

Thus, the drama of the *Laws* is to be found both through and within Plato's proposals for the new city state and in his critique of flawed governments. The latter shows that Plato was still hoping patiently, though in despair, to find the best specifications for the new city which in his eyes existed nowhere in reality. In order to find the latter, he used his poetic and dramatic powers in combination with philosophy, as he, better than anyone of his and possibly of our time, knew how to reconcile drama and philosophy.

My second chapter is concerned with the set-up of the state, and is mostly about how Magnesia would be organised and governed. I include discussions on the themes of women, homosexuality, marriage, freedom and education, and I discuss both the basic and the previous thought of Plato before considering his final thoughts, as expressed in the *Laws*. The reader is able to see clearly that the *Laws* is indeed Plato's only political work proper, an idea already expressed by my predecessors. It is a work based not on a utopian foundation but, conversely, offers a more realistic theory of state. I also believe that some of Plato's notions expressed here can be grasped and understood better if we compare them with those expressed in other dialogues, particularly *the Republic*, although under no circumstances should one regard Plato's views in the *Republic* as the sole foundation of his political philosophy.

In the third chapter, I consider the crucial religious aspects of the *Laws*. Here I am concerned with showing how Plato conceived the relation between man and God or Gods and with the validity of his demonstration of divine existence. I conclude that the *Laws* justifies the beginning of a new age, and that for Plato the source of the laws of any state is neither an anthropomorphic God nor man but a perfectly rational being. It is a being that has the power and ability to reason correctly and which by the use of reason can gain an understanding of the nature of what exists in the universe. What is striking is that Plato wants his rational being to understand that there is truth in tradition, that is, he wants to adopt the oral tradition although only to the extent that by combining it with his reason, he will be helped to arrive at the roots of human society.[26]

In this chapter I also include a section on Plato's last views on the existence of an evil kind of soul and on the role of pleasure in human life and the nature

---

[26] Plato, *Laws*, VI 752a.

of virtue, whilst showing that the role of philosophy is still important in the governing of the new state where the condemnation of sophistry is a must.

In my fourth chapter I portray the *Laws* as the first work in the ancient literature of what I shall term *dikonomia*,[27] jurisprudence. However, before I actually enter into Plato's notion of *dikonomia*, *I* feel it is essential to offer a brief preliminary discussion of the myth of the Furies. This is because I believe the latter to be the most ancient mention of *dikaiosyne*, as the punishers of those who committed homicide.

I also include in my discussion the relation between *agora* and *themis* and between *dike* and *dikaiosyne* in both the Homeric and Boeotian tradition, as well as after Homer. I also pay attention to how *dike* was viewed by the Presocratics, Theognis, Solon, Herodotus and by Socrates and the young Plato in particular, and consider the already existing dilemma of justice as found in ancient Greek tragedies, and those of Sophocles in particular.

In order to persuade his own society to adopt his set of laws, that he thinks are the best possible, Plato uses 'law' in many senses. He uses laws as instruments, as ends in themselves, and, more significantly, as *paideia* – teachers and parents. Plato thinks that society has its own *entelechia* (entelechy), that must lead to the fulfilment of a definite essence. This *entelechia* is nothing else but law itself, law being the ultimate result of the coincidence of civil society, state and ideal. Plato now understands why the rule of law requires the provision of an executive of magistrates, a system of *dikasteria* and a body of *dikasts*. He understands that the court is an agency of coercion and repression and should also have the related task of re-education. Moreover in the *Laws* Plato is the first to have drawn an explicit distinction between *ta idia* (private) and *ta demosia dikasteria* (public courts).

In concluding Chapter IV I offer a survey on Plato's view on punishment, additionally considering other dialogues where his theory on punishment was expounded and developed. In this way, I show that his view, like the majority of his views in the *Laws*, was a revised restatement of those expressed earlier in his career.

---

[27] *Dikonomia (dike + nomos* = justice, lawsuit and law). The modern Greek word *dikonomia* implies the totality of canons concerned with the procedures of trials (political and penal *dikonomia*). Even though the word occurs nowhere in the *Laws, I* felt it appropriate in order to describe what Plato is getting at in the work.

Chapter I
A Preface to the *Laws*

It is a fair presumption that until about 700 BC Greek culture was maintained on a wholly oral basis and that the Greeks of the Archaic period expected the epic and the lyric poets to perform the sort of role the mass media performs for us now. Even the Presocratic philosophers were essentially oral thinkers. This oral tradition of the Greek world developed into the different styles of tragic thought enacted in the dramas of Aeschylus, Sophocles and Euripides respectively. Aristophanes, in 405 BC – one year after the death of both Sophocles and Euripides and straight after the naval blockade and decisive defeat of Athens – writes in one of his prize-winning comedies, *The Frogs*,[1] that tragedy was dead, making it clear that one aim of comedy was to criticise tragedy and philosophy whilst entertaining the audience. Aristophanes ironically calls the dramatic poets 'the teachers of the citizens'. He tells us in the *Frogs* that Euripides in particular, whom he thought of as the worst among the Sophists, instead of making people better, led them to corruption and to a state of immorality and atheism.

Aristophanes, in his criticism of tragedy and especially of Euripides, alleges that the latter also allies with Socrates and that both men destroy the tradition of tragedy. However, it is hard, even impossible, to know for certain whether this parallel of Euripides and Socrates as sharing a radical and critical attitude to the traditions of the Greek world was actually Aristophanes' own impression and evaluation, or the expression of popular opinion. In any case, Aristophanes appears unwilling to accept the process of reasoning and the method of elenchus practised by Socrates, possibly due to his romanticism for the past or to his strong dogmatism. What Aristophanes failed to see was that the mission of Socrates, unlike his own, was not to entertain but to show his audience that with the power of reason they could offer rational answers rather than answers based on myths to the questions that had previously been

---

[1] Aristophanes, Frogs, 149a ff. Aristophanes makes the chorus state at the end of *Frogs* the actual cause of the death of tragedy. Dover, 1972, pp.172–189.

the concern of the tragedians. Although it is more or less true that at the time of Socrates and the Sophists the tragedians were indeed the most profound and active thinkers in Athens, Socrates dismissed them because he felt they had not and could not answer his questions. Plato could be said to have given birth at that time to something that Aristophanes never understood, and tried to offer an answer to the questions raised in Euripides' tragedies,[2] most notably in *Medea*,[3] where we hear Medea say, 'I know indeed what evil I intend to do, But stronger than all my afterthoughts is my Fury, Fury that brings upon mortals the greatest evils', speaking of her own *thymos* (anger) roused by Jason's desertion, and calls the latter the greatest evil to mortals, the most prevalent of human emotions.

At this point Aristotle is very relevant as he, too, in his *Nicomachean Ethics* supported the view that at the beginning of every action there is what he calls *proairesis* (choice)[4] the intent and ethics. For Aristotle, it is not the good intent that matters but the actual acquisition of the *agathon* (good). Thus, Plato, knowing that health is the most valuable thing in one's own life as clearly stated in *Gorgias*,[5] makes Eryximachus in the Symposium[6] say that one must control his *hedonai* (pleasures) so that he can avoid being ill, showing us that what might appear to be beautiful is not necessarily useful. Here, I feel we ought to parallel briefly the ideas of Socrates and Plato with that of St, Paul who claimed that, 'no one is willingly evil' and that we want to do certain actions but perform others. According to St Paul, the evil is rooted in our own nature. Our understanding knows what *agathon* is, but we do what we do, not actually what we actually wish, i.e. the evil. The cause of this is to be found in something 'dark' and metaphysical that we have inherited together with our body. Thus, for St Paul, the evil is inside us from our birth, in contrast to Socrates who thinks that we can escape from doing wrong when we receive the proper kind of education, as the latter believes in the human capacity to overcome evil. St Paul expects such help to come from the goodness of God. Aristotle[7], also, in his *Nicomachean Ethics* tells us that, when people become bad it is because of pleasures and pains, through seeking (or shunning) the wrong

---

[2] One of the questions raised by Euripides was that, '...we know what is good but we do not do it', as Phaedra states. The Attic tragedy dies with Euripides and dies because of Socrates, but with Socrates we have the birth of something new, that is, the birth of Attic philosophy.
[3] Euripides, *Medea*, 1078ff.
[4] Aristotle, *Nicomachean Ethics*, 1134a 1–3, 1139a 31.
[5] Plato, *Gorgias*, 451e.
[6] Plato, *Symposium*, 187e.
[7] Aristotle, *Nicomachean Ethios*, II, 1104 b 20–1105a9.

ones, or at the wrong time, or in the wrong way, or in any other manner in which such offences are distinguished by principle. Plato, continuing what Socrates had started – that is to help man to know himself, so that he can act consciously and discover the *agathon* rather that to promote *arete* by persuading men rhetorically – intends to teach *arete* and convince men rationally. Thus we hear in his *Apology* that he who wants to act correctly, like the heroes of Troy, and Achilles in particular, must not take into consideration the dangers that might occur.[8] In this light, Socrates was also in accordance with the poets Homer and Tyrtaeus, as he held that *arete* could also demand the sacrifice of one's own life. Apparently, Plato, in various of his dialogues, did offer answers to the question, 'what is *arete*?', and considered the latter as *andreia* (courage) *dikaiosyne* (justice) and *sophia* (wisdom). To suggest the inferiority of tragedy in the fourth century BC, besides Aristophanes' comments we may also rely on the comments of Aristotle. However, under no circumstances should one think that Aristotle's and Aristophanes' views belong to the same school of thought. Aristotle in *his Rhetoric*,[9] tells us that the success of a play in his day depended more upon the actor than the poet. This point is also raised in his *Poetics*.[10] Here[11] Aristotle also remarks that whilst the older poets made their characters speak like citizens, the poets of the present day make them speak like rhetoricians. However, Aristotle would not have been in agreement with Aristophanes' criticism of Euripides' as for him Euripides was 'the most tragic of the poets'. By this he meant 'the most powerful in arousing pity and fear'. Although Aristotle says that a good tragedy may have a happy ending, in the central part of his argument in *Poetics*, he nevertheless emphasises that the play which ends in misery is the most tragic and that this is the right ending. He concludes that Euripides, though to be criticised on other points, is supreme in this vital quality of the tragic.[12] This contrasts with Aristophanes' accusation of Euripides, partly because of the rather provocative ideas and philosophy that the latter embodied in his writings.

Aristotle's criticism of Euripides was limited to the more technical aspects of his plays. However, here we shall neither be concerned with the accuracy of Aristotle's criticism and specific comments on Euripides, nor with inconsistencies or obscurities that can be found in Euripides' writings. The evidence from Aristophanes and Aristotle shows that Euripides was considered suspect

---

[8] Plato, *Apology*, 28b.
[9] Aristotle, *Rhetoric*, 3.1.
[10] Aristotle, *Poetics*, c9.
[11] Ibid., c6.
[12] Ibid., 1453a.

by some of the educated Athenians' either because of his religious ideas and philosophy or because of the technical aspects of his plays, yet, for others, he was the philosopher of the stage. Moreover, whilst comedy was flourishing in Athens, Aristophanes through his comedies criticised the roles of tragedy and philosophy, and Socrates in particular. Plato was in some agreement with Aristophanes in that tragedy serves only for the pleasure *(hedone)* of the people. He described tragedy as a kind of flattery that does not lead to pure and genuine excellence *(arete)* of man.

Both Aristophanes and Plato based their criticism on their ethical views. What is also rather surprising is that even in Euripides there is the echo of that idea. We hear in *Medea* that the songs of the older poets in the *symposia* and other celebrations were merely intending to contribute to pleasure *(terpsis)* and not to the use *(kerdos)* of the unhappy.[13]

What one ought to conclude at this point is that there were discussions about whether the *agathon* of poetry was to be found in *terpsis or kerdos*, discussions that continue to occupy many scholars even in our time. Thus, Plato, living at a time that was marked by the rhetoricians Gorgias, Isocrates and Demosthenes, criticises the role of tragedy and rhetoric even in his early period dialogues, such as *The Gorgias*. Then, in the *Republic*, being aware of the educational system in Athens and knowing exactly what had happened and what was happening, he felt he had found a better way to teach, *(diapaidagogein)* the citizens of Athens in such a way that the traditional Greek myths would have no place in explaining the behaviour of human beings. Subsequently, Plato's criticism of poetry and his apparent hostility to it arose from his conviction and experience that all the existing educational systems in his time were flawed, an idea that he held until his last writing, the *Laws*. However, it is necessary to consider more carefully whether Plato was in any way actually hostile to poetry, and, if so, to what kind could he have been justified in his criticism if we consider the drama of the Greek cities of his time?

Plato's Criticism on Poetry

There is a tradition that Plato in his youth wrote tragedies which he then burned after deciding to devote himself to philosophy.[14] Although the reliability of this story is doubtful, we can at least be certain that Plato was writing as a philosophical dramatist throughout his career. However, Plato in numerous

---

[13] Euripides, *Medea*, 190–201.
[14] Diogenes Laertius, *Lives of the Philosophers*, *Plato*, chapter III, 2–6.

dialogues,[15] most notably in the *Republic*, offers his criticism on poetry arguing for an ancient quarrel between epic and dramatic poetry, especially tragedy, on the one hand, and philosophy on the other. What the existence of this distinction implies is that philosophy and poetry must have shared something in common in order for their conflict to take place. Generally, the themes, but not the characters, of Plato's philosophy were also the themes of literature: the relationship between man and God (indeed one of the main subject matters of the *Laws*), also that between nature and law, good and evil, freedom and necessity, those in and those under power, the limits of human initiative, the obligations and duties of the citizens in society, and the overall moral and political problems presented in social life. Thus, the battleground the two parties had in common was to be found in their themes, but in contrast to the dramatists who mainly drew their themes from legend – the stories of the Trojan War, of Agamemnon and of the house of Cadmus – Plato drew both his themes and his characters from his own life's experience in Athenian political and social life, using the character of Socrates as the main interlocutor in his dialogues.

Yet, I find Plato's drawing of this distinction between philosophy and poetry neither mistaken not provocative, as I see it as nothing more than a reflection of the distinctions between philosophy, history, science and imaginative literature that were emerging in his time.

The old Greek world of collectivism was gradually being replaced by individualism. In the early part of the fourth century BC in Greece, philosophy had become autonomous and was distinguished from both art and religion. If one considers Aristophanes' *Clouds*, though always with caution, one may see that in spite of his ironic jokes about Socrates in which Socratic philosophy is portrayed as representing all that was new and disturbing in contemporary Greek thought, philosophical speculation was of some interest to the Athenian public. This giving of some credit to philosophy must have encouraged Plato to draw his distinction.

The transition from drama to philosophy, as already cited in the previous section, had been heralded even in the plays of the tragedians. Thus, although I appreciate Plato's attempt to defend his native city, which was indeed the only city where this kind of Socratic philosophy could be developed, I venture

---

[15]Plato, *Euthyphro*, 6b–c; *Lysis*, 214a; *Gorgias*, 502d; *Symposium*, 223d; *Apology*, 22a–c; *Phaedrus*, 276e–277c; *Euthydemus*, 289c; *Ion*, 535 ff.; *Republic*, 376e–402, 595 ff., 606b–608b; *Cratylus*, 389a–b; *Laws*, 660a ff., 801c–802d.

There has been much scholarly discussion of Plato's criticisms. See, for example, Murdoch, 1977.

to say he was mistaken to despise the contributions of Homer and the dramatists to the education of the Athenians in a way that also implied the inferiority of drama to philosophy.[16]

Plato was well aware that drama had begun some hundred years before him, but felt it had failed to educate the citizen audience of Athens. This could of course be explained by the political factionalism that had made Athens into many cities rather than one. Hence, he felt it was the duty of his philosophy to help this audience turn away from their city and discover both their own true nature as well as that of the city, and consequently reconstruct the latter politically. But Plato's philosophical dialogues are not simply works of philosophy; they are works of a distinctive philosophical literature, works of drama made with the aim of edifying and instructing the audience and having a similar function to the one the poet had considered to be his. However, Plato, as shown in the previous section, does argue that the poets pronounce on life's problems without being able to offer an account either of themselves or their ideas. Thus, he complains they lack the true knowledge achieved by the philosopher who explicitly and systematically expresses his philosophical, religious and political thought. Plato aims always for a rational, explicable universe, in contrast to the tragic poets who felt that the universe was not like this. In this way, he portrays the poets as giving the wrong answers to the questions that had also been his concern, as they were operating at entirely the wrong level, presenting images of images rather than the world of reality and truth.[17] The poet, Plato tells us explicitly, does not even deal with the concrete and particular, but only with shadows and reflections, whereas dialectic like mathematics is concerned with the abstract and the universal. I am inclined to hold that it was his 'theory of forms' that helped Plato here to despise literature and put forward his criticism of poetry.

However, in spite of Plato's critical attitude to *poiesis* (poetry) he has often been misinterpreted as abandoning poetry and expelling the latter from his *Republic*, an interpretation not based upon what Plato wrote himself. On the first page of Book X of the *Republic*, Plato concludes that, '...we were entirely right in our organisation of the state, and especially, I think, in the matter of poetry... in refusing to admit at all so much of it as is imitative'. If we actually examine this sentence word by word we may see that it means that while Plato does not accept mimetic poetry in any way, he is not condemning all poetry.

---

[16] Plato, *Giorgias*, 502d. In particular where tragedy is regarded as essentially a kind of rhetoric. See also Plato, *Republic*, 607b–608b.
[17] Plato, *Republic*, 597e.

Even in the famous passage that has led to the impression that Plato rejects the poets completely, it is important to note that he rejects not every poet but only the mimetic ones.[18] On the contrary, he explicitly declares that the poet exercises a very valuable function in *orthe polileia (kallipolis)*[19] and that, 'Our poets must compose hymns suitable to the marriages that then take place'. He goes on to say that,

> if a man, then, it seems, who was capable by his cunning of assuming every kind of shape and imitating all things should arrive in our city, bringing with himself the poems which he wished to exhibit, we should fall down and worship him as a holy and wondrous and delightful creature, but should say to him that there is no man of that kind among us in our city nor is it lawful for such a man to arise among us and we should send him away to another city after pouring myth down over his head and crowning him with fillets of wool, but we ourselves, for our souls' good, should continue to employ the more austere and less delightful poet and taleteller.

He adds that the function of the poet is, '...to imitate the diction of the good man and would tell his tale in the patterns which we prescribed in the beginning when we set out to educate our soldiers'.[20] Thus, at this point he apparently includes even the mimetic poetry to some extent. What he excludes is the mimetic poetry that expresses 'a character of necessity and variety', and, if I may say so, one cannot entirely avoid the problem of Plato's inconsistency here. However, the later exclusion of the poet who imitates everything does not mean that Plato does not appreciate the success his own works might have had with the public, which is a paradox of course.[21] What is Plato doing, writing mimetic dialogues?

The criticism of the content of poetry in the *Republic* is demonstrated by the speech of Adeimantus.[22] However, this was also expressed in other Platonic works which could be said to have prepared much of the ground for his criticism of poetry in the *Republic*, though poetry is not the main concern of Plato in this work. It is, nevertheless, related to his notion of education, as it is one of the effects of the latter.

---

[18] Plato, *Republic*, 398a.
[19] Ibid., 459e–460a.
[20] Ibid., 398a–b.
[21] Ibid., 387b.
[22] Ibid., 362d–367e.

In the *Laws*, a work also concerned with finding a way to educate its audience, Plato, in considering the nature and purpose of education, shows how the arts should reinforce and serve education. He sees the importance of the arts which reinforce the discipline of the feelings of pleasure and pain in a man's life and which form the habits of liking and disliking the appropriate things.[23] This is also what Aristotle thought of education when he described it as learning to feel pleasure and pain about the proper things.[24]

Although the Athenian regards the arts as a very important factor in the service of education, he is still cautious about them, demanding that the legislators make arrangements for the proper supervision of poets and musicians. To justify the validity of this point, he refers to the conventionality of Egyptian art,[25] showing that just as the Egyptians had stereotyped their art and allowed no deviation from fixed forms, so the Greeks could have artistic conventions, though not necessarily the same ones as in Egypt.

Yet, poets in Magnesia will be under the lawgiver's direction in order to persuade the citizens of what the good life is, and to convince them that the just man is always happy.[26] Thus, Plato is no more and no less sympathetic to poetry in the *Laws* than in the *Republic*, but in the *Laws* the function and contribution of the arts in the cultivation of a child's moral sense through its taste and imagination is treated at greater length than in the *Republic*. Plato still advocates some artistic censorship and the maintenance of a correct standard of taste, in all that concerns drama and the arts. However, what is worth stressing is that in contrast to the *Republic* where responsibility for the establishment of the state is the true *logos*, in the *Laws*, apart from the general theoretic thoughts there is also a historic illustration whose main source is Homer.[27] In the *Laws*, Plato argues for a minister of education who is to be the premier minister of the community. We may conclude that Plato, aware that poetry formed a part of the Greek tradition of educating the young and knowing the failure of Athens, felt the need to put across in the utopian *Republic* his pragmatic criticism on poetry. By doing so, he showed his own educational objectives whilst emphasising the wrongfulness of the quality of the existing educational system in his own native city. I believe that one should see Plato's apparent attack upon the core of Greek literature not as a way of allowing him to exercise a monopoly with his own school of thought,

---

[23] Plato, *Laws*, 653.
[24] Aristole, *Nicomachean Ethics*, 1104b, 11.
[25] Plato, *Laws*, 656d–e.
[26] Ibid., 659–600e.
[27] Ibid., III 680d,e.

but as a way of helping his audience to acquire knowledge 'of what things really are' and to distinguish their reality from their appearance.

This educational objective of Plato remained the same until the end of his career, as the *Laws'* critique of various educational systems shows; the need to impose restrictions upon poetry is still there.

On Reading a Platonic Dialogue

Broadly speaking, the number of people who read Plato is quite limited, and more questionable is how many of those who read his writings actually understand what he meant by them. Consequently, it is not surprising that the products of scholarship generated by the works of Plato, have caused great difficulties of interpretation throughout the subsequent centuries. However, a common theme often expressed in many current readings of Plato is the dramatic interpretation of his dialogues.[28] Allan Bloom, Paul Friedlander, W.K.C. Guthrie, Werner Jaeger, Jacob Klein, Stanley Rosen, F. Schleiermacher, Leo Strauss, and V. Wilamowitz are a few among those who have attempted to interpret the dramatic elements and form in Plato's dialogues though often in a brief and general way. Yet, there have been others like F.M. Cornford, Sir Karl Popper and, more recently, Julia Annas,[29] who have omitted all the dramatic passages from consideration, and indeed, this is the basic failure their interpretations share. The latter interpreters will not occupy our attention here except incidentally. This does not mean, however, that the three interpreters cited above did not offer valuable philosophic insight in their discussions of such dialogues as the *Republic, but* it means that their interpretations were flawed by their neglect of the dramatic aspects of Plato's works.

Before I move on to emphasise points of vital importance, already illustrated by my predecessors who have indeed showed awareness of the dramatic elements of the dialogues, I must apologise to all those I have missed out of my list. I consider it essential to acknowledge the contribution of those with whom I am familiar – in spite of the risk of appearing a bore who explains what has already been explained – as I do not intend to take complete credit for such an interpretation. Schleiermacher[30] was one of the first to rebel against the earlier attempts by many interpreters to abstract doctrines

---

[28] Bloom, 1968; Friedlander, 1969; Guthrie, 1978, pp.321–82; Jaeger, 1943, vol. II; Klein, J., vol. 2, no. 3; Klein, J., 1965; Rosen, 1968; Schleiermacher, 1815; Strauss, 1964; Wilamowitz, 1919.
[29] Cornford, 1935; Popper, 1966; Annas, 1981.
[30] Schleiermacher, 1815.

(dogmata) from the dialogues in order to build a system. He instead insisted on the need to study Plato's artistry, indeed a point of vital importance. I, too, conceive Plato's dramatic art as serving his philosophy, and his dialogues as dramas having a philosophic purpose. This blending of philosophy and drama was appreciated also by Jaeger,[31] who paid great tribute to it in his *Paideia*, and by Klein.[32] The latter, whilst speaking about the *Philebus* notes that, 'A Platonic work is usually a drama or mime in which what happens cannot be separated from what is said and argued about.'

Friedlander,[33] discussing the character of the dialogue as a mode of philosophic presentation, states that, 'Plato may still rightly be called the creator of the philosophical dialogue as a genuine work of art comparable to the tragedy and comedy of the preceding age', while Bloom,[34] in his preface to the translation of the *Republic* in which he discusses the general character of the dialogue form, notes that, 'We then have Plato the poet and Plato the philosopher, two beings rolled into one and coexisting in an uneasy harmony ...Every argument must be interpreted dramatically and every dramatic detail must be interpreted philosophically ...Separately these two aspects are meaningless, together they are an invitation to the philosophic quest,' while Klein,[35] commenting on Plato's *Meno*, writes that, 'it seems it is not enough to talk about the dramatic character of the Platonic dialogues from the outside.' Meanwhile, Leo Strauss,[36] in his essay on Plato's *Republic*, writes:

> one cannot understand Plato's teaching as he meant it, if one does not know what the Platonic dialogue is. One cannot separate the understanding of Plato's teaching from the understanding of the form in which it is presented. One must pay as much attention to the *how* as to the *what*. At any rate to begin with, one must pay even greater attention to the 'form' than to the substance since the meaning of the 'substance' depends on the form. One must postpone one's concern with the most serious questions (the philosophic questions) in order to become engrossed in the study of a merely literary question. Still there is a connection between the literary question, and the philosophic question.

---

[31] Jaeger, 1943, vol. 2, pp.78–80.
[32] Klein, 1968, vol. 2, pp. 157–158.
[33] Friedlander, 1969, pp.157, 161.
[34] Bloom, 1968, pp.xv–xiv.
[35] Klein, 1965, pp.5–6.
[36] Strauss, 1964, pp.52–59.

The study of the literary question is therefore an important part of the study of what philosophy is.

Rosen,[37] in his discussion of the *Symposium*, stresses the significance of the dialogue form. He tells us that, 'especially among English-speaking writers the emphasis upon epistemological and linguistic analysis had directed attention away from standing dramatic form, and toward the dissection of particular themes, or arguments in relative independence from their context. Instead of a vigorous attention to the dramatic context of an argument as a key to Plato's intentions – and here as an essential part of an argument itself – we are presented with speculations about the chronological order of the dialogues...', and 'In general if we reduce the dramatic structure of the dialogues to the status of an external contingency, we arbitrarily ignore their most obvious and pervasive feature. Even without entering into any theoretical reflections on Platonic dialectic it is clear that we cannot take the dialogues seriously as expressions of Plato's thought unless we take seriously the extraordinary complexity of the literary form.'

Wilamowitz[38] ought also to be mentioned as he has suggested that the purpose of the early dialogues is poetic and imaginative – not profound or philosophical – in short, that the purpose is dramatic, a view that was also expressed by D. Hyland.[39]

However, none of the interpreters cited above, though contributing substantially to an understanding of Plato, and raising valuable and illuminating points, have gone far enough in either (a) looking at dramatic elements rather than seeing the dialogues as dramas as a whole, or (b) paying attention to works like the *Laws* alongside the early and middle dialogues.

I am approaching the dialogues here in what I conceive to be the most appropriate way – that is, dramatically – and considering the *Laws* as drama, though I understand that its subject matter is about laws. I hold to the view that my predecessors have proceeded with their analyses of Plato's dialogues using a mistaken methodology – considering the subject matter of the dialogue only. Take, for example, Rosen, who despite his concern with the dialogue form considered the *Symposium* as a work about love. *Timeaus* has also often been viewed as being a work about cosmology, especially by Cornford, the *Republic* as a theory of totalitarianism as by Popper, and the *Laws* either as a

---

[37] Rosen, 1968, pp.xi–xiv.
[38] Wilamowitz, 1919, vol. 1, pp.1–3.
[39] Hyland, 1968.

theological poem or as the most mature work of political philosophy by Voegelin and Strauss respectively. However, none of the Platonic dialogues has been considered as a drama proper, that puts forward compelling issues arising from the real drama of humanity. In this way, examining it closely and not treating it simply as a ploddingly written work but understanding and taking it seriously, we could solve the disagreement among commentators as to which is the best way to interpret the *Laws*, a method that could also be applied to all other Platonic dialogues. In interpreting the dialogue as drama, I do not wish to imply that Plato simply wrote literature; rather, I am suggesting that he wrote a unique form of literature which he blended masterfully with philosophy and vice versa, a literature in which the philosophical issues are expressed dramatically whilst the drama of his works covers philosophical themes such as those we now term cosmology, epistemology, metaphysics, a theory of justice, penology and jurisprudence. The prevailing view is both confusing for readers and wrong in itself as it makes Plato like a caricature, abstracting and then attaching special features of a dialogue, generalising them, and consequently building a system which may be beautiful but would always be partly or wholly unfaithful to what the dialogue aims at giving us. The dialogues, in my view, ought to be read as a series of planned, carefully designed philosophical discussions that carry Plato's central ideas to explore his reasons for believing what he does through his extremely careful presentation of arguments rather than his attempt to create doctrines. Whether the dialogues were actually written or simply delivered orally, we cannot know. What we may know is that they were written for a particular audience. *Phaedrus*[40] the most introspective dialogue, confirms this, implying that Plato was aiming to make his views public. Thus, each dialogue should be read as a separate work, a single discussion aimed at getting its audience to think about a different subject. However, this does not mean that a dialogue necessarily had only a single theme or subject. It could be composed of various discussions, each on a different subject and yet all interrelated; therefore it ought to be read and approached in a particular way, one that extends beyond what we now term Socratic elenchus and which reflects the face than that anyone's reading of a Platonic dialogue should be based on Plato's own text and have the intention of inviting people to stimulate discussion.

Let us now point out some details about the *Laws* which may challenge the current understanding of the dialogue as the least important and least dramatic in the Platonic corpus, and as containing a very small number of philosophic

---

[40] Plato, *Phaedrus*, 277.

arguments. At this point I must also point out that it is wrong in my opinion, though it is almost given in Platonic scholarship, to divide Plato's dialogues into periods and attempt to date them. The date of the dialogues is not of primary importance. Certainly, during his life and career there were changes in society and so there was necessarily a development of his thought. The content of Plato's dialogues does not, however, necessarily require a connection with time. And since we cannot actually tell when the dialogues were written exactly it is wrong to read them as a unified whole, as scholars like Paul Shorey have demonstrated.[41]

The *Laws* as a New Kind of Drama

> Most honoured guests, we're tragedians ourselves, and our tragedy is the finest and best we can create. At any rate our entire state has been constructed so as to be a 'representation' of the finest and noblest life – the very thing we maintain is more genuinely a tragedy. So, we are poets like yourselves, composing in the same genre, and your competitors as artists, and actors in the finest drama, which the law alone has the natural power to 'produce' to perfection (of that we are quite confident).[42]

According to the text of the *Laws*, as the Athenian says at this point in the discussion, the interlocutors' task was similar to that of tragedians. However, under no circumstances should this be taken to mean that Plato in the *Laws* accepts tragedy in its current form. He is still apprehensive about the inclusion of the tragedians and their tragedies in the new state. He considers it essential to appoint authorities to decide whether 'the work of the tragedians would be fit to be received and suitable for public performance'. What Plato must mean, when he describes their discussion as the most beautiful, the best and the truest tragedy, is to point out to the tragedians that it would be essential for their works to be of philosophical character in order to be allowed to be performed in Magnesia. The ideas expressed in tragedies should be expressed in a rationalistic form of philosophy similar to the one adopted in the *Laws*.

In short, Plato attempts to demonstrate that philosophy is still primary in his thought, whilst suggesting to the tragedians the basic model or the best prototype upon which their works should be based. Thus, I take the *Laws* as

---

[41] Shorey, 1946, p.xxxii.
[42] Strauss, Leo. 'Plato', in *History of Political Philosophy*, edited by L. Strauss and J. Cropsey. Chicago: University of Chicago Press, 1987.

Plato's intention to replace the old kind of tragedy, which by the second half of the fourth century had become politically, morally and ontologically corrupt, by a better kind of philosophical poetry. The latter was not based on the theory of forms, but it described a city in speech evidently more attainable than the utopian *kallipolis* of the *Republic*.

Aristotle in his *Politics*,[43] in spite of all the deficiencies he finds in the *Laws* as in any other 'Socratic discourse' and his disappointment that the *Laws*' greatest part is in fact about laws that say very little about the constitution, nevertheless describes the *Laws* as '...brilliant, original and with an urge to investigate ...and that is beyond measure'.

However, on the whole, modem scholars do not take into serious consideration either Plato's own remark that the *Laws* is 'the truest and best tragedy', nor Aristotle's assessment and understanding of the work. Nevertheless, I find both remarks about the *Laws* acceptable enough for reasons I shall explain shortly. Yet, I am aware that Strauss, Voegelin and Pangle are three amongst other philosophers who have attempted to do justice both to Plato's comment and to Aristotle's understanding and criticism of the *Laws* in order to keep the spirit of the *Laws* alive. Strauss[44] defends the *Laws* as a mature work of political philosophy. He writes that the *Republic* and *Politicus* lay the foundation for answering the questions of the best political order, the order best compatible with the nature of man, but they do not set it forth and that this task is left to the *Laws*. The *Laws* is thus Plato's '...only political work proper; it is his political work par excellence'. However, Strauss views the *Laws* as being not merely political, as he believes that it also contains 'Plato's theological statement par excellence'.

For Voegelin,[45] the *Laws* is Plato's '...mature wisdom on the problems of man in political society'. It describes a city ordered according to '...the quality of men whom Plato envisaged as the vessels of the idea'. Voegelin also agrees that the *Laws* is more than a political work: 'It is a work of art; and specifically it is a religious poem in which every fact and argument adduced serves its purpose in adding to the grand view of human life in its ramification from birth to death'. It is the *'summa* of Greek life', as Voegelin points out. A close examination of the work, as well as of the Athenian, Spartan and Cretan societies, confirms this. It shows that most of the laws described in the dialogue are copied from laws, expedients, customs, regulations and codes

---

[43] Aristotle, *Politics* 1265a 12–14.
[44] Strauss, 1973, p.78; pp.29–31, 134; chapter 1.
[45] Voegelin, 1957, pp.3, 216, 219, 222, 228.

already in force in all three societies mentioned above. The best reading for a historical interpretation and valuation of the Platonic *Laws* is undoubtedly Morrow's book *Plato's Cretan City*, where he justifies the above point.

Pangle[46] also writes that the *Laws* '...is far more than a set of speeches about law through the interaction of the characters. Plato intends to show how a philosopher might win the confidence of powerful old political leaders and guide them towards a revolutionary regrounding'. He adds that the drama of the dialogue reveals the 'degree to which theory and the human type that embodies the life of reason can guide political practice'.

All the above prescriptions do help the reader gain access to the world of the *Laws* and thus enlarge his philosophical interest in it, but they are not always in complete agreement with my understanding of the dialogue; even though I, too, think highly of the *Laws*, I do not understand it simply as either a theological, a political or a philosophical matter. Part of my purpose in writing about the *Laws* is to stimulate thinking about its drama, both in form and content, attempting to justify as uncontroversially as I can that it is a work of literature that absorbed tragedy into a vision of ethico-political philosophy. It is a work that suggests that ancient political philosophy and dramas mainly concerned with moral questions do go together, to the effect that neither of them can be grasped or evaluated without reference to the other.

Diogenes Laertius[47] tells us of the development of philosophy in relation to tragedy:

> But, just as long ago in tragedy the chorus was the only actor and afterwards, in order to give the chorus breathing space, Thespis devised a single actor, Aeschylus a second, Sophocles a third and thus tragedy was completed, so too with philosophy: in early times it discoursed on one subject only, namely physics, then Socrates added the second subject, ethics and Plato the third, dialectics and so brought philosophy to perfection.

Indeed, the *Laws* implies the mutual interdependence and link between Greek drama and political–ethical thought. These parallels and continuities between tragedy and political–ethical theory could well be found even in other Platonic works like the *Apology*.

---

[46] Pangle, 1980, XI cf. 377.
[47] Diogenes Laertius, DL3, 56.

My main argument of the *Laws* being 'drama' is based on the following four assumptions: first, in the use of the dialogue form; second, as in a true religious drama there is the divine background; third, it covers similar themes to those of tragedy; fourth, a number of themes are woven together so that there is an 'interplay' of themes comparable to the interplay of characters if not necessarily of themes in a play.

At this point I ought to bring into my discussion Bloom's[48] understanding of Plato's use of the dialogue form. He writes that many modern interpreters of Plato make a 'fatal error' in attempting to separate the form and substance of the dialogue. Similarly to Bloom, I, too, believe that it is wrong for anyone to attempt to separate them, as they both have the same end, that is, they both intend to offer an intellectual training whose end is the acquisition of *phronesis and sophia*. In the case of the *Laws*, is true to say that its literary manner, based on the dialogue form, should be examined alongside the theme, substance and purpose of the work. Yet I must also make my position explicit here in that I will be using the term 'drama' both in the technical sense as well as in the looser sense of 'the drama of human life'. In short, the term will be used both for form and for content in order to avoid any hostile critic who may complain that I am using it in more than one sense.

In order to achieve his proposed aim in the *Laws*, Plato makes use of his familiar dialogue form, which is not arbitrarily chosen. The use of the dialogue form is described by the Athenian as the 'most well measured' of all Greek poetry and prose. He goes on to say that there is no better, example (*paradeigima*), than it *for paideia and poiesis (*education and poetry*)*.[49] He hopes that in using the dialogue form the interlocutors will acquire moral and dianoetic virtues and that it will help make their thinking harmonious. In the first phase of the dialogue, Plato, as in other works, does not centre it on the substance of the problem but simply stresses elements that, though partly related to what will follow, do not contain the problem. It must be noted that although on the whole the interlocutors who appear in the beginning of a dialogue are not usually the most important people of the group in that dialogue, this is not the case with the *Laws*, as the interlocutors are the same from the beginning of the discussion right to the end. However, as with other dialogues, once the Cretan and the Spartan have stated their positions we have the Athenian's intervention that aims at proving that their views expressed before were based on a false logic and so were not the right answers. They are

---

[48] Bloom, 1968, Preface.
[49] Plato, *Laws*, VII, 811d.

thus led to the second phase where the same question is taken up again, and this is followed up by other phases, each contributing something more to the progress of the discussion. The use of different phases in the *Laws* is more evident than in other works and helps to direct discussion in an ethical way until the solution is found, that is, until agreement has been reached as to the legislation for Magnesia.

Yet I appreciate that, in general, a Platonic dialogue reaches its philosophical peak when Socrates argues against his stronger opponent or when there is a myth in the dialogue. Indeed, in a number of dialogues the interlocutors who start the discussion gradually disappear from the dialogue. Their absence is not so apparent because they are replaced by interlocutors who have more positive views and offer solutions to the problems they themselves are concerned with. This is not the case with the *Laws*, as the discussion is of a different style aimed at improving the audience by teaching them the proper way they should adopt rather than placing emphasis on particular individuals. Besides, that was the purpose of tragedy, and so Plato correctly regarded *the Laws* as a true tragedy because reason was considered from the point of view of ordinary citizens.

The fact that the interlocutors are not tragic themselves is similar to many plays where the characters portrayed by the actors are not tragic themselves. Also, as in a true religious drama, there is the divine background in the *Laws*: 'Tell me, gentlemen, to whom do you give the credit for establishing your codes of law? Is it a God or a man?' asks the Athenian. 'A God, sir, a God – and that's the honest truth. Among the Cretans it is Zeus; in Sparta – which is where our friend here hails from – they say it is Apollo, I believe. Isn't it right?' replies the Cretan Kleinias.[50] Indeed the dialogue starts with the question of the Athenian concerning the cause of their laws. However, the purpose of their discussion is not mentioned in the beginning of the dialogue but at the end of Book III.[51] Both his companions consider them to be of divine nature. The Cretans attribute them to Zeus, the Lacedaemonians to the God, Apollo. It is noticeable that *theos* (God) is the first word of the *Laws*, whereas in the *Apology* of Socrates it is the last. In the *Apology the* conclusion of the speech of Socrates ends with the word *theos*, that is an indirect indication of his unjust offence about *asebia* (impiety, disrespect) and *atheia* (atheism). In the *Laws*, Plato starts his discussion with *theos* in order to justify the wrongness

---

[50] Plato, *Laws*, 625a.
[51] Ibid., 702b.

of the Sophists' belief that laws were separate from it. Laws for Plato were of *theion* (divine), divine nature and inspiration.

'What is the purpose of the state and legislation, courage or *arete* as a whole?' The Athenian asks his interlocutors. Indeed this question characterises on the whole the discussion that follows a discussion concerning government and laws and requires the identification of the actual incoming of the state whilst considering some of the main customary laws of the Dorian cities. According to the two representatives of the Dorian cities, it is to prepare their citizens for war in such a way that other cities would be afraid of their power. The Cretan Kleinias states that the natural condition of the relations between states is not peace but the *akeryktos polemos* (undeclared war).[52] Although the Athenian appreciates the polemical and military character of the cities (Sparta and Crete), he thinks that they overdevelop and promote only one single *arete*. For the Athenian the *eudaimonia* of a state is not to be found in its cultivation of a single *arete*, but in the promotion of *aretai* in general. Moreover, the Athenian stresses that the purpose of legislation is not war but peace and that instead of cultivating only courage, they should have laws that would care about making all the citizens *eudaimonas*, by offering them all the goods.[53]

The Athenian distinguishes *agatha* in two kinds: divine and human. Only when a state accepts the divine ones, will it obtain the human as well – otherwise it will have neither the former nor the latter. The most important of human gifts are first, health; second, beauty; third, physical power and fourth, wealth – not base or meaningless wealth, but the wealth that is based on *phronesis and nous*.

Of the divine goods, first comes *phronesis*, second, *sophrosyne*, third, justice and, fourth, prudence. The divine attributes are superior to the human ones. Thus, the legislator must legislate considering the divine goods as primary, and the human as secondary.

Plato then expresses his doubt of whether pleasure should be included in human life. He shows his apparent disagreement with the Dorian legislators who excluded drinking parties and *symposia*. The exclusion of the latter in their states did not make their citizens *sophron;* on the contrary, the people's inexperience of what the measure of pleasure should be often led them to excesses of pleasure. What Plato states here is that the *symposia* are in fact an

---

[52] Plato, *Laws*, A 626a.
[53] Ibid., A 631.

exercise for enkrateia (self-control) and *phronesis* (prudence).[54] In this way, the Athenian shows the superiority of the divine goods to the human ones and the divine origin of the existing laws in the sense that they were thought to proceed directly from a God.

Although the Athenian does not wholeheartedly accept this view, he nevertheless walks together with his companions in order to arrive at the cave of Zeus. The latter could be said to be the real focus of the divine element in the dialogue.[55] Besides, the path the three interlocutors take from Knossos to the sanctuary of Zeus is the same path that the legislator and King Minos used to take every ninth year when he met his father Zeus in order to be advised on his legislative work. However, the three interlocutors never reach the cave of Zeus. That could mean either that they had already reached God up to a certain level or that the cave of Zeus would be of no relevance to them as they had discovered other means in order to legislate for the new state. Whatever the truth is, the *Laws* could be viewed as a religious drama as, similarly to the latter, the Gods do not appear but are in the background. This is in contrast to a drama in which the Gods do appear in the play. Also, as in many plays where the Gods do not control what the actors do and suffer, here, Plato makes his three characters reach agreement as to which would be the best laws for the new city without actual interference from any God, though always keeping the divine element behind any law, in the sense that the laws chosen as a whole were either related or leading up to an understanding of the existence of divinity.

The scene of the dialogue is set on the island of Crete,[56] which may indeed surprise the reader as most of Plato's dialogues were set either in the Athenian *agora* or in the houses of Plato's own friends. Certain clues suggest that events in Sicily had influenced Plato at the time of the writing of the *Laws*,[57] and thus the reader might have expected the discussion to be set there. The dialogue's setting in Crete could be explained by Plato's lack of interest in existing states which he believed to be all bad. Besides, Crete was thought to be the initial

---

[54] Plato, *Laws*, A 637a.
[55] Nilsson, 1950, pp.53–68, 272; Marinatos, 1940–1, pp.129–36; Plato, *Laws*, 624a; Plato, *Minos*, 3196.
[56] Morrow, 1960, chapter 1.
[57] Plato, *Epistle* VII, 331e–332e. It must be noted that the Seventh Epistle is the longest and most valuable of the Platonic letters, having the best claims to authenticity. Even critics who reject the authenticity of most of the letters have accepted the seventh one as genuine Plato. In this letter, Plato gives a detailed account of his dealing with Dionysius the Younger, explaining his motive to go to Sicily and participate in the political affairs of the latter, and the reasons for his failure to carry out his plans.

source and centre of Greek civilisation from Neolithic times to the late Bronze Age; the whole civilisation of the Bronze Age has been called Minoan, after the Cretan king Minos. All the legislators who followed in Crete, as well as that of Plato in the *Laws*, were inspired by Crete. Moreover, it has been argued that whereas the Dionysiac cult came from Thrace, the Orphic Cult came from Crete, even though it bore strong Egyptian elements. So, knowing that the Orphic cult was of Cretan origin, Plato chose Crete, since he admired and was influenced by it – as many of his works, the *Laws* in particular, show.[58]

The characters are three elderly men, Kleinias, a Cretan; Megillus, a Spartan, and an unnamed Athenian. Both Kleinias and Megillus represent the Dorian tradition that, according to Plato, *eunomountai amphyteroi*, but they nevertheless represent an improvement over the legislations current in their states, by avoiding being biased. I take the unnamed Athenian as a fictionalised Plato or a misguided Socrates. Plato could not have used Socrates in the *Laws*, as it is known that Socrates had never left Athens, except when necessary for military duties. Moreover, Plato in the *Republic had* represented Socrates as the spiritual founder of the *aristes politeias*, the *kallipolis*, that was first in excellence and first in order. The city of the *Laws* is the second best of the ideal city and is distant from the *idean tes poleos* (ἰδέαν τῆς πόλεως). Similarly, the Athenian stranger of the *Laws is* different from either the Platonic or real Socrates and the ideas expressed in the *Republic*.

The characters are presented as old men, possibly due to Plato's intention to stress their wisdom. What their age shows also is that although old, they were still looking for the best policies to be adopted by the new state, thus making their drama stronger, whilst showing that old age was a necessary requirement for one who would direct and participate in such an inquiry. Similarly, in the *Republic* the guardians do not undertake ruling until the age of fifty. The nationality of the three characters is due to Plato's intention to test the best of the Dorian against the best of the Athenian laws and institutions. This, in return, presumably explains at least in part the dialogue form. The subject of the discussion is apparently about government and laws. It is indeed a subject that reflects the various attempts of human beings to find out how a city may approach the unattainable end of political partnership and how it would be possible to found a city with the best possible political institutions and laws. Yet it is a subject that shows how human beings may recognise the nature of their mortality, the limits of their humanity. Above all, it shows

---

[58] Plato, *Laws,* 657a–d, 677d, 715e, 716a, 735a, 782d, 819b–d. See also Plato, *Minos,* 318b.

Plato's thinking about the relationship between God and human being, a theme of many tragedies where men had also aspired to be Gods yet understood the nature of their mortality. However, the fact that they are three characters trying in different ways to find the best laws, implies that none of the three states represented had such laws. The three interlocutors, therefore, could be seen as each representing the 'drama' of his state, thus making the drama of the laws as a whole, strong and powerful.

The Athenian leads the discussion, and he is really more important than his companions. That Plato often severely limits both the Cretan and the Spartan contribution to the discussion, or even keeps them silent altogether, is not, I believe, due to a lack of ideas but is part of his implicit rule for a successful enquiry. Also, it may be part of his intention to help the audience see for itself the flaws, if any, contained in the interlocutors' arguments.

Having set the scene, the characters and the subject of the discussion, Plato makes them *thaumazein* (wandering). The process of *thaumazein* had also been mentioned in *Theaetetus:* 'The sense of wonder is the mark of the philosopher. Philosophy indeed has no other origin'.[59] It was also expressed in Aristotle's *Metaphysics:* '...all men commence their inquiries from wonder whether a thing be so, as in the case of the spontaneous movements of jugglers' figures to those who have not as yet speculated into their cause.'[60] Aristotle argues that philosophers marvel at the fact that all things are as they are. It is through wonder that a human being begins to philosophise, first by wondering about perplexities and then by degrees raising questions about such matters as astronomy and the genesis of all things. This process of wondering is in fact characteristic of all human beings, showing the drama of human nature and life. However, what is interesting in the *Laws* is Plato's understanding that apart from what we may call ontological or critical philosophy there is also the human phase of philosophy where its principle and subject is man. Philosophy in this phase is born not simply with wandering or with doubt but with the understanding of the dependence of man and the conditions of his life, such as evil, faith, death and so on, as man is apparently free and yet always dependent on something else. Plato here intends to combine theoretical with practical

---

[59] Plato, *Theaetetus*, 155d.

[60] Aristotle, *Metaphysics,* book I, chapter II, 982b. What Aristotle means here is that whereas the old kind of philosophy originated from wonder – that is, ignorance – and attained unto a sort of knowledge, when men reached this knowledge, knowledge as such became the great actuating motive in speculation. Current science (metaphysics) would set out from an opposite point in this progress, because of starting from the consideration of that which is the highest object of speculative knowledge.

philosophy. He begins with a theoretical question in order to show the spiritual passion of the interlocutors for knowledge, wisdom and philosophy. In doing so he hopes to enable the interlocutors to come to a state of knowing themselves first, as well as showing awareness of the laws and institutions current in their states, before deciding what laws would be best for others.

In showing the drama of human nature and affairs that he sees to be the outcome of their relativity and instability, and so stimulate pity and fear in the audience as a tragic play would do, he is helped by his use of history in Book III.[61] The latter has often been considered the earliest example of the philosophy of history in the literature of the ancient world. Even though here we will not be concerned with how much of Plato's account is reliable, that is, with his reliability as a historian, it will be of some interest briefly to compare Plato and Hegel in their view of philosophic history, though it must be noted that Plato never explicitly formulated such a theory.

Hegel[62] writes that philosophy dwells in the region of self-produced ideas, without reference to actuality, whereas history is subordinated to what is given, to the realities of fact and that this is its basis and guide. For Hegel, philosophy does not give any real guidance to the real life of mankind, but only has to conceive what appears in the formation and maturity of historical reality. Philosophy, for Hegel, is subject to history and is not simply an Epimethean self-knowledge of the history of reality. Plato also constructed what we now call philosophy of history, in Book III. Here, in particular, he never made philosophy 'sink' into the 'tide' of the philosophy of history. For Plato, philosophy is the Promethean apocalypse in mankind, making demands that define the fulfilment of man's life both in its individual track and in its social plot.

We see that Plato makes his characters enter into direct discussion of what the nature of political organisation is and how it arises. However, as the Athenian knows that there is no reliable evidence about the beginning of civilisation, he attempts to represent it imaginatively whilst stressing that, 'the old stories must be perfectly credible to any man'.[63] This oral tradition said that in the past there had been many cataclysms from which only a limited number of people managed to survive. Amongst those who survived were mostly those who lived in the mountains and such men must have been in general unskilled and unsophisticated.[64] In this period life was based on the

---

[61] Taylor, 1960. See also St Augustine's *De Civitate Dei*.
[62] Hegel, Introduction: 'Reason in History'.
[63] Plato, *Laws*, 677a.
[64] Ibid., 677b.

family and the leaders were the eldest, whilst the status quo was that of *dynasteia* (δυναστεία), based on customs and ancestral laws.[65]

In the following stages, life was based on common customs. One of these was the choice of leaders and of legislators, whilst the form of government was either aristocracy or kingship until it became that of democracy.[66] At this stage, where he describes the three phases of Greek society, the Athenian philosopher is like a pupil himself.[67]

One needs to remember that in *Protagoras*,[68] where also Plato mentions the myth of Prometheus, he tells us that '...men lived at first in scattered groups. They were not cities. However, they sought therefore to save themselves by coming together and founding fortified cities'.[69] And since Zeus was concerned with the future of the human race he sent Hermes to bring to the humans '...the qualities of respect for others and a sense of justice'.[70] He tells us both in *Euthyphro*[71] and the *Laws* in particular that, 'Justice is said – and well said – to be the daughter of Respect, and both are the natural scourges of falsehood'.[72] On the order of Zeus, those two *aretai* were attributed to everyone whilst he told Hermes that, 'There could never be cities if only a few shared in these virtues, as in the arts. Moreover, you must lay it down as my law that if anyone is incapable of acquiring his share of these two virtues he shall be put to death as a plague to the City'.[73]

Other sources which bear witness to the tradition Plato is using here as regards the absence of legislation and justice in the first and second stages of social changes are Herodotus,[74] Theognis[75] and Thucydides.[76] Herodotus, when he talks of the race of *androphagoi* (cannibals), tells us that '*oute diken nomizontes oute nomo oudeni chreomenoi*'. Theognis tells us that, 'Kurnos, the city stands; her men are changed. You know, in former days, there was a tribe / Who knew no laws nor manners, but like deer / They grazed outside the city

---

[65] Plato, *Laws*, 680a.
[66] Ibid., 680d.
[67] Ibid., 627a.
[68] Plato, *Protagoras*, 320d–322a.
[69] Ibid., 322b.
[70] See also Hesiod, *Works and Days*, 256–257.
[71] Plato, *Euthyphro*, 6a.
[72] Plato, *Laws*, 943e.
[73] Plato, *Protagoras*, 322d.
[74] Herodotus, IV 106.
[75] Theognis, *Elegies*, 53–57.
[76] Thucydides, in the introduction of *The Peloponnesian War*, B15, 2.2; Plutarch, *Theseus*.

walls and wore the skins of goats'. Also, Thucydides in his history tells us that in the place that is now called Greece there were not permanent dwellings and that citizens were often forced to emigrate by bigger groups of people. In another passage he notes that originally in Athens the citizens lived *kata komas* with their own *boulefteria* and *prytaneia*. It was Theseus who later connected all the different *komai* and made them have a single *boulefteria* and a single prytaneian.

Plato, in the *Laws*, could rightly be said to offer an account of what we term imaginative prehistory, and though not factual it nevertheless shows the endless search by human beings to survive and find the best possible conditions that will allow them to live happily.

However, what the reader should realise at this point is that even though we may find this an apparently causal explanation of events, when Plato explains the gradual formation of city states his concern is not so much the causal aspects (that people, for example, had to stick together in large political entities in order to survive) but the teleological aspects. It was 'by nature' necessary that they should reach the form of a political community, because a political community is good in itself. The sequences are more simply temporal rather than causal: a certain time is needed for the ideal to actualise itself, and this is precisely what Plato is describing in Book III of the dialogue. He then puts the theoretical drama into more practical terms – possibly due to his wish for his reform to be carried out, perhaps in an actual Greek state or in a Sicilian town if the latter were to be restored after the death of Dionysius. Thus, he passes from theory into practice in the sense that his imaginative prehistory is now replaced by actual facts. He tells us about the foundation of the Dorian confederacy of Sparta, Argos and Messene, whilst showing us the example of a constitution that had withstood time, that of Sparta. In this way, he shows the tragic drama of both Argos and Messene where there was a concentration of sovereignty in the same hands which led to their fatal failure. In Sparta, on the other hand, there was a division of power which could be found in its dual kingship; the institution of Gerousia and the Five Ephors. Even though Plato disagrees with many elements of this system, he praises it, as he sees an ideal separation and harmonious function of its organs which are balanced against one another.

Book III is indeed the place where the tragedy of human life is evident, as Plato shows us how all three states had begun in a promising way by establishing laws prescribing the rights of kings and peoples respectively, but it was only Sparta that survived, possibly because the laws enforced in Sparta were 'stable',[77] the Athenian tells his companions. Thus, in order to avoid a destruction of the city for which he is now legislating, he uses history in order to make the interlocutors recollect how things had been and thus make them respect what had proved to work. He prefers to find the new state on safe grounds and so forms it on the Spartan model. However, this is not to say that he does not mean that the Spartan constitution in itself would not be somehow injurious for the new state. What the state actually needed was a well-proportioned mixture of despotism and democracy that would inevitably produce the best constitution and would help to avoid excesses.[78]

After Book III, a kind of catharsis sets in, which, even though it does not come at the end of the work, helps the audience to be purified from the pity and fear arising from the preceding account of history. It becomes evident as soon as the three interlocutors are given the task of legislating for Magnesia. They deal with institutions and laws concerned with the political and ethical well-being of its citizens, and so search for the best laws and institutions. Indeed, by the end of the work they have found the best conditions under which Magnesia is to be founded and so the dialogue does not have an aporetic ending.

It is true that the characters are not as vividly portrayed as in early dialogues, and also true that in the *Laws* there is less give and take than in the former. Yet it is also true that even in the *Republic*, which is often considered as dramatic Platonic dialogue, after Book I there is not so much conversation, and the role of Socrates' interlocutors is not different from that of the Athenian and his companions. In both works, the interlocutors have a function which is both a part of and yet slightly separated from the main arguments like the chorus' function in a tragedy that is both a part of and yet slightly separated from the main action. Even though I also appreciate that many passages in the *Laws* are rather ploddingly written and there are some inconsistencies I nevertheless hold that the original aim of Plato is passed on successfully to the audience. The reader should not be concerned with how many digressions or inconsistencies are contained in the *Laws*, as inconsistencies there can also be found in tragedies, but rather whether Plato passes his thoughts on to his audience. And in examining closely the *Republic*[79] one may see that there are more inconsistencies there than in other Platonic dialogue. Also, the fact that the *Laws* contains conclusive positive teachings and is not

---

[77] Plato, *Laws*, 797a.
[78] Ibid., 639d.
[79] Plato, *Republic* V, in particular. See also Halliwell, 1993, pp.1–29.

aporetic does not make the dialogue less dramatic either than other Platonic works of art, or the famous works of the dramatists that also contain conclusive positive teachings. Inconclusiveness and *aporia* do not make *Republic* I, for instance, more dramatic than the rest of the work, or the first three books of the *Laws* less dramatic than the rest of the work where *aporia and thaumazein* are replaced by a different philosophical method which revolutionises men's souls and blossoms into a garden of questions concerned with the way men should live. Thus, I consider the *Laws* to be just as dramatic as other Platonic works or works of the dramatists and most precisely as a drama where a number of themes are woven together so that it contains a theory of a new state. The *Laws* is concerned with politics, as well as ethics and the individual, and, above all, with a theory of jurisprudence. It is a drama with a mixture of themes whose real unity is to be found in God. It is God who holds all the parts together and God who is beyond all of them. In this way, there is an interplay of themes that could be comparable to the interplay of characters if not necessarily of themes in a play.

However, all the above descriptions are subordinated to its drama; they are the teachings which emerge from its dramatic reading. They are simple teachings, describing an everyday reality and so intended to suit an average citizen, similarly to the institution of tragedy that is suited to an average citizen and aimed to educate him. But this Platonic tragedy, though comparable to those of the dramatists, is of a different kind, a kind that has *proper paideia* in its heart rather than a work that would simply arouse emotion, that is, mostly pity and fear, until the catharsis[80] takes place. It is a work that shows that pity and fear can be avoided if the individual knows how to use his reason properly, an attempt to provide stability in the *Laws* and in the literature of the new state. Plato's aim is to help his audience to get rid of its passions, as the latter were the curse of man, leading him to a state in which he was acting entirely without reason: a man without reason was simply a slave of his emotions. Plato's aim, as already stated above, was not the intensity of the emotions of his audience, as for him life was neither a vale of tears nor a land of smiles.

---

[80] Aristotle, *Poetics*, v10–vI7. 'Tragedy is, then, a representation of an action that is heroic and complete and of a certain magnitude – by means of language enriched with all kinds of ornament each used separately in the different parts of a play: it represents men in action and does not use narrative, and through pity and fear it effects relief to these and similar emotions.'
See also Plato, *Republic*, x 595a–608c, where Plato talks about the emotional effects of art as nourishing the lowest part of the soul. Indeed in the *Laws* this arousal of emotion is replaced by stimulating reason,
Murdoch, 1978, pp.40–42, and Annas, pp. 335–354.

Life for Plato was to be found elsewhere, in the power and stimulation of reason that would help man to develop his moral consciousness. Indeed, the *Laws* is a tragedy that challenges both traditional and sceptical treatments of the Gods and of Greek tragedy in general. It is a debate about the archaic, aristocratic and democratic worlds, and their means for the education of their citizens. Thus, its stress is neither on the greatness of the heroes and their deeds nor on the idea of the association of the Gods with implacable punishment of men's wrongdoings, nor with radical scepticism about the Gods, but with a mode of rationalistic thought. It is a tragedy that is concerned with the *eudaimonia* of human life and not with the preservation of tradition. Plato was well aware that from the beginning of history man had known only one tragic world and had not been capable of stepping out of it. However, he knew well that when an empire falls, the life of the individuals should continue to progress, gaining new experience whilst understanding what had gone wrong and led to the decline. From his own experience, he knew that the fall of an empire was due *to its paideia*, hence the definition of *paideia*[81] as being that which helps man reason correctly in order to preserve the superiority of *nous* and *nomos*. *Paideia* is the first indication of *arete* which shows man how to tame his *thymos*, desires, and that in order to acquire *arete* he must have a healthy judgement and natural *logos*.[82] In that way, the individual will lead both himself and his state into a state of good government and true political freedom. The latter comes across by the individual's mixture of the following qualities: *nous* (mind, intellect), *metron* (measure), *aidos* (respect), *deos* (fear), *philia* (friendship), *eleftheria* (freedom). Indeed, the *Laws* was such a text, was based on the mixture of all the above qualities and as such it ought to be included in the new state or be adopted in the educational system of other existing states.

---

[81] Plato, *Laws*, 635b–c.
[82] Ibid., 653d.

Chapter II
The Organisation of the State

The Place of Magnesia in Plato's Thought

Turning then to the *Laws* we find that the greater part of it is in fact 'laws' and he has said very little about the constitution, which in spite of his wish to make it more generally acceptable to actual states, he gradually brings back round again to the earlier one. For apart from the sharing of wives and property, he constructed the two constitutions on very much the same pattern: the same kind of education, the same life of freedom from essential tasks, and the same arrangements for common meals except in the *Laws* women also are to have common meals, and the number of those bearing arms is five thousand not one thousand.[1]

In spite of the fact that modern scholarship on the whole does not agree with Aristotle's appreciation of the *Laws* and its relation to the *Republic*, I think very differently and hope to demonstrate this in the chapter that follows.

In the dialogue *Politicus*[2] Plato notes that:

among forms of government that one is pre-eminently right and is the only real government in which the rules are found to be truly possessed of knowledge, not merely to seem to possess it, whether they rule by law or without law, whether their subjects are willing or unwilling, and whether they themselves are rich or poor – none of these things can be at all – taken into account in any method.

In this work[3] Plato also declares the importance of observing laws as the means of avoiding violence in the state. In this way he raises respect for the laws into

---

[1] Aristotle, *Politics*, 1265a 1. See also Plato, *Laws*, 737e, 781; Plato, *Republic*, 423a.
[2] Plato, *Politicus*, 293c, 294a, 303b.

an ethical–political demand, whether these are written or just customary. Then in the Laws,[4] confirms the worth of the *Republic* as the prototype and tells us about his ideal state, where there is neither private family, nor individual private property, and where instead of written laws there are the philosopher–kings, the incarnators of the ideas of the *kallipolis*.[5] However, the state he is constructing in the *Laws* is not based on the unfettered discretion of the rulers so evident in the *Republic*, and even though Magnesia might be less noteworthy than the *kallipolis*, it is closer to reality than the latter; a historically realistic state in that it is not based on the ideal qualities of the philosopher–kings. It is something in between ideas and reality, like the ideal state of the *Republic*, in so far that it would not be so easy to put it into practice since it is actually based on some powerful circumstances which do not exist in reality. For this reason, even this 'second best' state is no more than another piece of Plato's advice to his fellow citizens, telling them of their imperfections and weaknesses. What is true in Magnesia is that Plato no longer places emphasis on the presence of the philosopher–kings, who have an understanding of the ideas, and the form of the good in particular, and so could distribute justice in every way having the latter as their criterion for doing so. In contrast, he now proposes laws which leave a certain measure of freedom to the practitioner. Thus, in the second best state there will be neither an extreme of despotism, as in the case of Persia, nor excessive liberty as in Athens; there will be neither full freedom nor insufficient freedom for the practitioner of the laws. There will be neither full knowledge of every proposed law, nor full ignorance of their very existence and aim, as Plato now, in contrast to the *Republic*, allows the possibility of knowledge to every individual, an idea that becomes evident throughout the dialogue.

Thus, laws are to be drawn up in such a way that they will not be imposed on everyone without an explanation of their cause. In other words, before every legislative order there will be a sort of introduction to all the reasons for the necessity of the proposed law. And it is indeed with the help of these preludes that Plato proposes making the laws important instruments in the education of those under their authority in the best state, and at inculcating moderation. Plato now replaces the absolute authority of the philosopher–kings and their unfettered discretion, awarding some independence to the individual, and thereby limits to some extent the right of the state to be the

---

[3] Plato, *Politicus*, 300b–c.
[4] Plato, *Laws*, 739a–740a.
[5] Plato, *Republic*, 739c.

only arbitrator of justice. It is essential, therefore, for the legislator to come close to reality and attempt to combine the authority of man with that of the state, and the freedom of man with the demands of absolute government by the state. As such, Plato has to find a way to combine democracy with monarchy in order to give a more fair and balanced form of government, so that the state of the Magnesians derives all its authority from the mass, and establishes the democratic principle of mass sovereignty. Plato goes further, so that on top of the will and authority of the masses there will be a more powerful will, that is, the will of law. Only from within the framework of law shall the will of the people have validity. What is more important is that the will of law can neither be destroyed nor be changed by the masses. This is the monarchical element of Magnesia in the sense that the law is the monarch.[6]

The Material Assumptions for the Establishment of Magnesia

In the *Republic*[7] Socrates recognises that the *kallipolis* is a pattern formed in heaven, which anyone could see and establish in himself. However, he does fear that without the ideal environment, the individual's efforts face the greatest difficulties. In the *Laws*,[8] too, before offering his legal, social and administrative prescriptions for Magnesia, he is primarily concerned with finding a suitable environment that must not be by the seashore, and yet be Mediterranean. Plato suggests that the sea leads a person towards trade and inevitably into becoming a profiteer, so that his ethical and political education is made more difficult. It is also important to find the best suitable citizenship for Magnesia. Plato doubts whether it should be made up of one nationality of the same origin, language and customs, since the proposed laws would meet with resistance from citizens of the same nationality who would already have their own customs. Also, he wonders if the population of Magnesia should be made up of people of different nationalities and origins so that the people would not resist the proposed laws, as none of the latter would have existed before in any of the state. Above all, he understands that in this way, the psychological element that the consciousness of one nation would presumably tend to support its own customs and principles, would be absent.

However, Plato does not offer a firm answer to this question. In addition to a suitable citizenship there is a need for exceptional personalities to become the first legislators and governors of the new state. He adds here that it would

---

[6] Plato, *Laws*, 875e.
[7] Plato, *Republic*, 592c.
[8] Plato, *Laws*, IV.

be better if it could be a philosopher working together with an absolute ruler. This principle is to some extent a revival of that expressed in the *Republic* about the necessity for philosophy and politics to coincide. Indeed it was also expressed in other earlier dialogues, most notably *Gorgias*,[9] where Socrates regards himself as one of the few, indeed the only one who has the right attitude to politics rather than being involved in practical politics.

In the Seventh Epistle,[10] Plato also tells us, 'In the days of my youth my experience was the same as that of many others. I thought that as soon as I should become my own master I would immediately enter into public life'. However, the principle of the *Laws* is at the same time somewhat contradictory to that of the *Republic*, in that whereas in the *Laws* the philosophers have to work with the rulers, in the *Republic*[11] the rulers should be philosophers, a principle contradictory also to Plato's original proposal in the work, that one person should do one job.[12]

Plato next moves on to regulate the arithmetical number of the population and in doing so he bears in mind two criteria: first, he considers how many people can be supported in the Spartan way, by the cultivation of the land, and second how many will be needed if the state faces an external attack from possible enemies. He uses the hypothetical number of 5040 citizens (*politai*). Indeed, this is a number not arbitrarily chosen for, if analysed, it is a convenient and yet useful number because it has 'the most numerous and most consecutive subdivisions and is most suitable for administrative purposes both in peace and war.[13] The number 5040 is a number multiple divisible by 12; according to the Pythagoreans' 12 was the symbol of the *arche*, (corresponding also to the months of the year, the Zodiac and the Sun) which is the measure of time, illuminates the notion of the same, and provides knowledge of number. The land is divided into lots of equal value, and every citizen, together with his family, is given one, so that he may possess modest estates whilst also being allowed to have his private family. In order to keep the social balance, the size and number of families should not increase beyond the proposed number. If any do exceed the number quoted above, the state must move them away, establishing colonies and so making them emigrate. Thus the principle of equal families and equal lots will be preserved and so the land

---

[9] Plato, *Gorgias*, 521d.
[10] Plato, *Epistle* VII 324.
[11] Plato, *Republic*, 472c.
[12] Ibid., 433a.
[13] Plato, *Laws*, 737e, 738a, 771b.

will remain divided and will not be gathered in the hands of a few, as had happened before when Solon was required to put forward his reforms.

There is a currency that circulates in Magnesia, but it has value only in Magnesia itself and not in the whole of Greece. Gold and silver exist too, but are meant to be the possession of the state which will use them in dealings with other countries or to give to individual citizens with permission to travel outside the state.

The Magnesian Social Classes and the Continuation of Plato's Social Philosophy

As Plato is interested in the preservation of unity and harmony in the state, he once again puts forward his social philosophy, already central in the *Republic*.

In the *Republic* there are three social classes:[14] the guardians or the ruling class, the auxiliary class and the productive class. However, it is fair to say that most of Plato's recommendations in this work concern only the ruling class, i.e. the governors and their auxiliaries, the police soldiers, whose members, both men and women, possess complete political authority in return for which they live a garrison life with no private property or even private families.

The other members of the state, that is, the productive class, are simply concerned with offering their best services to the state, mainly as farmers and artisans, and have no part in decision-making or even the administration of the state. Moreover, they are not entitled to receive any higher education. The latter plays a great part in the life of the guardians, and it is through this intellectual training that some of them will become philosophers, and thus be the true philosopher–kings of the state.

The *Republic* shows Plato's belief that these three classes correspond to fundamental faculties in the human soul: the rational which commands, the spirited which attacks, and the appetitive which desires.[15] Wisdom controls the first, courage the second, and temperance is a harmony of all three, very close to justice. The latter is the disposition of all to harmonise under the rule of wisdom. Hence, the wise state is a state where wise guardians ensure mediation and reconciliation among the classes beneath them.

In the *Laws*,[16] Plato develops his social philosophy further, in spite of the fact that the social structure of Magnesia is different from that of the *kallipolis*, which depended both for its creation and for its presentation upon its kings

---

[14] Plato, *Republic*, III.
[15] Ibid., IV.
[16] Plato, *Laws*, 744–745a.

being philosophers or philosophers being its kings. The state of Magnesia is composed of guardians, citizens, artisans, metics and slaves, whereas in *the Republic*, slaves are assumed in addition to the three classes and there is also no mention of metics.

Plato further divides the Magnesian citizens into four property classes, as he is aware that there is bound to be some inequality of wealth. This division is due to his notion that every citizen will contribute money and services to the state according to the social class to which he belongs, In a similar way, penalties will be imposed upon criminals, according to social class and political status, and this reminds us also of the principle imposed in the *Republic* of treating equal people equally and unequal unequally. However, it must be noted that in the *Laws*, Plato puts limits on wealth, laying down the inequalities that lie between a minimum and a maximum limit of wealth. The maximum limit is four times the value of the original lot, and whatever one earns above that limit will be possessed by the state. The 5040 citizens of the state are thus required to work only on their farms and are forbidden to engage in commerce which could well involve selling, like the productive class of the *Republic* whose main mission was to be farmers and artisans, but essentially not sailors with their trading activities.

The citizens of Magnesia are offered an intensive programme of state education which is compulsory, starting from the age of three.[17]

Apart from *the citizens* in the state there also live the metics, but these are not granted permission to live in Magnesia for an indefinite period. The state, Plato holds, allows them to live there on the assumption that they will exercise some useful art. Magnesia thus differs from ancient Athens, where metics were allowed to live for an indefinite period. Here, Plato allows them to stay for twenty years only, but this can be extended if they satisfy the proposed requirements. Their main purpose is to relieve the citizens of certain tasks so that the latter can work and hold various posts such as doctors, nurses, craftsmen and teachers. One wonders what the real difference is between them and the citizens, if they can both do the same jobs, possibly equally well? The metics may indeed be acting at much the same level as the citizens' but the state can welcome them for the fulfilment of its social or moral purposes, and unlike the citizens, they have no political power and no say in the government. Above all, the state can expel them, or, if they prove to be good, as long as the state has not grown too large, it can extend their stay.

---

[17] Plato, *Laws*, 850a.

Plato also understands that there will be some temporary visitors to Magnesia too, comprising *xenoi* and *epidemoitntes*. Indeed, he describes four categories.[18] There will be traders, visitors to the religious festivals, official ambassadors from other states, and private philosophers who will come to commune about the eternal verities with the high officials of the state.

Plato's attitude to *xenoi* is not clear. On the one hand, he argues for treating them with respect and consideration since Zeus, the God of strangers, watches over them and so they must have a special position in the state.[19] On the other hand, he goes on to say that they will import foreign customs into the state which might be harmful and destructive.[20] There will also be slaves in Magnesia who will be owned by both citizens and metics. The majority of these will be employed on the farms and in the fields and will generally do all the manual work. Plato here expresses an existing Greek idea; his recommendation about the inclusion of slavery was no more than what was actually current practice in the states of the Greek world. Slaves were recognised as a species of property, and accordingly many could be bought and sold in the market.[21] However, Plato holds that they should be treated firmly and humanely, and that although a man should not become close and familiar with them, he should not treat them badly either.[22]

The area in which we see the main difference between the *kallipolis* and Magnesia is in their political construction, and the ruling body in particular. In the *Laws*, there are thirty-seven *nomophylakes*[23] that make up the main instrument of its political power. This body of men is charged with the ultimate supervision of the *Laws* and, along with the other guardians of the state, it provides the ritual substance of the state. The *nomophylakes* make certain that the *Laws* are being preserved, whilst controlling the wealth of the citizens and placing them in the proper class accordingly. As there is the principle of popular sovereignty in Magnesia, the *nomophylakes* are elected by the citizens.

The election takes place in a rather complicated way. Only those people who have fulfilled their military duties have the right to vote. They elect three hundred *politai*, and there then follows a second ballot in order to select one hundred out of the original three hundred. Next, a third ballot chooses the thirty-seven *nomophylakes* out of the one hundred. There is also an advisory

---

[18] Plato, *Laws*, 952d.
[19] Ibid., 729e.
[20] Ibid., 952e.
[21] Ibid., 916a ff., 936c–e.
[22] See also Aristole, *Politics*, 1255b 30.
[23] Plato, *Laws*, 752e–753a ff.

body that helps the *nomophylakes* and this is composed of three hundred and sixty members – ninety members from each class.

Paideia in Magnesia

In the *Republic*, Plato recommends that education ought to be employed as the chief method of reforming both the individual's character and the state. He tells us that in a just character, each of the three faculties he has found in the soul and the state is exercised to the height of its power:[24] reason recognises what is good, the appetites freely conform, and the ability to enforce the dictates of reason assures that conformity. In a just state, each adult citizen performs the function for which he is best fitted: the highly rational engage in legislation, the predominantly spirited enforce it, and the chiefly appetitive operate the economy. Thus, each fraction refrains from interfering with the functions of the others. Reform in the individual character and in the state is a movement towards personal and social justice.

A system of universal, compulsory public education, from birth to maturity, needs to be instituted to bring about this individual and social improvement. However, it is not in fact clear in the *Republic* whether all citizens receive the education described or only the future guardians. Moreover, it is not explicit whether some should learn the art of war and others should study the sciences and dialectic – the search for the fundamental principle that explains all reality and value. What is explicit, though, is that Plato holds that each class in the state would be recruited from those best fitted to perform its function; such a system of education would produce individuals whose souls are as just as their faculties allow, and a state whose parts or classes are similarly harmonious. So, if we ask why every human being should possess the three abilities (reason, spirit, and appetite) and why every class should perform one of the three functions (legislation, law enforcement and economic production), the answer is that they cannot fail to follow what is required by the forms. But of course, one could justifiably object that this is a circular argument and that Plato also makes a mistake in treating people as if they were cities and vice versa.

What I wish to highlight here are some features contained in Plato's view of education, that are also apparent in the *Laws*, so that we may perceive the connections between his theory of education in both works. First, we note Plato's authoritarianism,[25] as early education at least is to be all about forming

---

[24] Plato, *Republic*, 441e.
[25] Annas, 1981, p.89.

good habits rather than self-expression or creativity. Second, there is the important idea in the *Republic*[26] of 'turning the soul around', so that education on the higher level is not putting knowledge into people but enabling them to see things for themselves. Third, we ought to note that Plato provides equal educational opportunities for men and women, making education compulsory and, above all, controlled by the state.[27] In the *Laws*, education becomes more lenient and flexible to some extent, though the principles of the *Republic* are still operative and education remains first and foremost the concern of the state. However, the method Plato adopts here is different, as education is now not only the concern of the state, but also of the family, though always under the rules of the state. The basic difference is that education in the *Laws* is not based upon the form of the good. Plato does not place his entire emphasis upon the highest stage of educating the rulers. Education is extended to all citizens, no longer restricted only to the two higher classes as in the *Republic* – probably due to Plato's wholehearted attempt in this dialogue to voice popular current views and sentiments. Although the details of how the lives of the young should be organised are discussed rather vaguely in the *Republic* – in the *Laws* they are given in more detail. Education, as Plato defines it, is '...that training in virtue from childhood which makes man eager to become a fully-fledged citizen knowing both how to rule justly and how to obey'.[28] Education aims at developing in the child the qualities of mind and character that most fully express the idea of human nature. A sound system of education requires the integration of intellect and emotion.

The idea expressed in *Republic* VII explains why, in the introductory books of the *Laws*, Plato attacks aspects of the education systems in the Dorian states. Although the *Republic*[29] had to some extent welcomed Spartan influence, Spartan institutions are now under suspicion and are criticised.[30] Plato is being self-critical here – just as in other late dialogues such as *Parmenides*, *Theaetetus* and the *Sophist* of the *Republic's* metaphysics and epistemology. Jaeger[31] saw the

---

[26] Plato, *Republic*, VII. Education is not, Plato says, a transfer of knowledge into the soul, like putting sight into blind eyes; it is more like turning the eye to the light (518c). All the educator can do is to provide the conditions in which the right kind of mind can develop its capacities.
[27] See Annas, 1981, pp.79–101.
[28] Plato, *Laws*, 643e.
[29] Plato, *Republic*, 544e–544b. Plato describes the Spartan timocracy as the real-life constitution that came closest to the ideal.
[30] Most notably in books I and II of the *Laws* where Plato discusses the aim of Spartan and Cretan laws and the educational effect of drinking parties (637a ff., 641a ff., 645d ff.).
[31] Jaeger, 1943, vol. III, p.219.

Laws as the best commentary on the *Republic*. In the first two books of the *Laws*, Plato refutes the Dorian ideal of life taught by Tyrtaeus' poems and adopted in both the Spartan and Cretan institutions that portrayed life as war.[32] For Plato, whenever men think victory is the only thing worth living for, courage inevitably becomes the only virtue. The reader at this point needs to remember that Plato himself in the *Republic* described the Spartan constitution as the existing constitution that came closest to the ideal. He now takes up the old dispute between Tyrtaeus, who praised courage, and Theognis, who taught that all virtues were comprised in justice, and he decides in favour of Theognis.[33] Men had to learn that courage in conjunction with other virtues, that is, justice, self-control, and piety, is better than courage alone.[34] Plato thinks that Tyrtaeus ought to be 'corrected' by Theognis and that legislation must be directed to produce a more whole virtue.[35]

Positive human attributes such as health, strength, beauty and wealth are to be subordinated to the four virtues of the soul which Plato calls divine goods.[36] Plato shows how legislation can bring about and cultivate one particular virtue by describing how courage had been cultivated in Sparta and Crete by the institution of *syssitia* (messes), common for men, and by physical exercise for military purposes, by hunting and by all sorts of hardening methods. Yet the Spartan system of instilling courage teaches its pupils to resist fear and pain but not the temptations of pleasure, and Plato notes that it is this error that makes them surrender weakly to lust. Of course there is a conventional element here, as historians such as Xenophon and Plutarch tell various stories of Spartan generals or kings being easily bribed and the like. Plato here tells us that the Dorian system has absolutely no institutions to cultivate temperance and self-discipline.[37] The influence of the *syssitia* and organised games in this direction is doubtful.

The Athenian speaker cites the Dorian love of boys as an unnatural and degenerate form of normal sexual life and criticises the sexual looseness of the Spartan women.[38] The Spartan prejudice against wine and drinking parties does not seem to him the right way of teaching self-control, but, rather, is a shameful way of turning one's back upon lack of self-control. A love of wine,

---

[32] Plato, *Laws*, 629a–631.
[33] Ibid., 692a, 630a–c.
[34] Ibid., 630b.
[35] Ibid., 630e.
[36] Ibid., 635b–d.
[37] Ibid., 635b–d.
[38] Ibid., 836a–837a.

like so many other things in life, is itself neither bad nor good. Plato suggests that there should be rigid discipline at banquets supervised by a good chairman to bind the wild and chaotic elements into a cosmos. The point he is attempting to prove here is that *symposia* are beneficial if they are conducted in a fine academic spirit.

Plato starts the discussion by offering his criticism of the Spartan tradition whilst elaborating on his own thoughts *about paideia* (about education) and the training of desires in particular. In this sense, I believe his educational theory turns out to be a continuation of his previous theory, as expressed in the *Republic*, since he still aims to educate the desires of his citizens. However, even though in the *Republic* the whole of *paideia* is based upon the form of the good and the entire emphasis is placed upon the highest stage of it, in educating the rulers, in the *Laws* he begins with earlier childhood.[39] He now understands the necessity of explaining the psychological basis of education so that it begins by moulding the unconscious self. He is now interested in showing how the rational and conscious aspects of *paideia* (its truly philosophical elements, one might say) come straight from the pre-rational and subconscious or half-conscious levels of the life of the soul. This idea was suggested in the *Republic*, but it is interesting to note that Plato in the *Laws* concentrates very hard on discussing how it is psychologically possible.

The principal necessity *in paideia*, he now holds, is proper pre-school training, and so he starts his discussion by investigating the development of desire in childhood, examining how the pleasure–pain principle which is particularly strong in children can be used in the service of education. In Book VI[40] he tells us that the two partners in a marriage are to believe that its highest social purpose is the creation of children who are as good and as beautiful as possible.

Plato advises expectant mothers to take long walks, and after the baby is born to 'shape' it like wax with massage – up to the age of two.[41] The mother is to carry the baby in her arms on country walks and to the temples, visiting relatives, until it can stand by itself. The reason why Plato here proposes walks to the temples for the baby is that, for him, the early years of childhood are indeed the most formative ones. When he says that the baby should exercise even in its mother's womb, that is only an extension of physical education, thinking that when we give a child comfort and abolish discomfort by the

---

[39] Plato, *Laws*, 643b.
[40] Ibid., 775d–776a.
[41] Ibid., 789a–793.

movement of its body, we have taken the first step to moulding its soul. It is because Plato thought that all education was moulding the soul that he was the first to establish an educational system for early childhood, conceiving of education as a process involving the whole person. This is what Plato thinks will be attained by giving a baby exercise when it is still very young.

Depression and anxiety help to create fear. Habit is a very powerful thing. Plato actually says that *ethos* (character) is derived from ethos (habit). The child in his first three years is dominated by pleasure and pain and Plato thinks that children must learn to feel these and to love and hate them appropriately. When they grow up, they will come to understand the reasons underlying the training they have received.

A sound system requires the integration of intellect and emotion, and Plato's solution is to divide education into stages. From three to six, children ought to do nothing but play. Only if a child is too sensitive or cowardly should he be punished, in such a way that he does not harbour resentment but does not get off scot free. Life should be made pleasant for a young child, but not to the extent that the child becomes a pleasure glutton. The officials who supervise the children should encourage them to develop the maximum degree of skill and versatility in the use of both hands and feet. If possible, all children should grow up ambidextrous. From six months onwards, boys follow lessons and girls may too, if they have the inclination. The children will learn to dance and to wrestle. The boys will also learn the use of weapons and the skills of armed combat. The games the children play and the dances they learn will be fixed by being made sacred; they must not be allowed to vary randomly. Varying the games children play has an effect on character-development; once the fight games have been determined, no casual change is to be permitted. Games and dances are to become part of religion.

The general curriculum Plato proposes for Magnesia is derived directly from the one proposed in the *Republic* for the education of the guardians. In the *Republic*, only the ruling class and their auxiliaries need to be trained for military service; in Magnesia, all citizens will be expected to defend the state if the need arises. In the *Republic* the third class of citizens has no real need of systematic education, having no part to play in political decision-making and administration, while in Magnesia the entire body of male citizens shares in important decisions and nominates and votes for officers of the state: all these citizens need an education similar to that of the auxiliaries of the *Republic* and this is precisely what Plato proposes. He argues that all citizens should educate their desires by themselves rather than placing the task entirely upon the rulers and auxiliaries.

Even though Plato appears to be more 'open' towards the arts in the *Laws* than in the *Republic*, he still remains convinced of the need for stern censorship of the arts – he is opposed to citizens acting in tragedies and comedies, and to trivial versatility in musical performance.[42] In short, he suggests complete state control of all education, publishing, and all other means of forming public opinion and the individual character. For Plato, uncontrolled poetic inspiration should not have any place in a rationally ordered society, as it implies a moral and intellectual danger. I believe that Plato would not approve of the freedom that there is in our mass media and the destructive effects this has upon the young in particular. The equivalent effects upon the young in his time came from the stage which tended to impress and even indoctrinate youth.

Drinking parties and public amusements were to be strictly regulated. The fact that Plato does not examine the question 'why do people drink?' is because in his society *oinos* meant something different. Besides, Plato's concern was to regulate the social rituals of drinking, not to restrict the market for wine. Trade in Magnesia was to be kept at a bare minimum. Although drunkenness was discussed in Plato's time and later, it cannot be compared with the addiction of man to alcohol today. Nowadays, people drink because of their sorrows or out of their boredom, and a certain percentage of people who drink are motivated to drink by advertising. Yet, to put strict rules on alcohol, or ban it altogether, is rather impossible as this would violate current international free trade agreements. Nevertheless, it is true that a certain percentage of car accidents is caused by drunken drivers, but alcohol, as already stressed, cannot be banned, and if anyone attempts to ban it, he will soon be called authoritarian, totalitarian and so forth. This is also the reason why twentieth century interpreters of Plato think of him as such. However, the mistake they all make is that they don't place Plato in his own time, but in our modern materialistic and capitalistic world. Moreover, Plato suggests that the *Laws* itself should provide a useful and exemplary text book for literary study;[43] he suggests that the minister of education[44] should ensure that similarly valuable examples of verse and prose writing be sought out for pedagogical use, and that the conversations, discussions and speeches of the kind recorded in the *Laws* be committed to writing to become texts for study.

---

[42] Plato, *Laws*, 816–817e.
[43] Ibid., 811d–e.
[44] Ibid., 765d–766a.

Teachers are expected to learn texts in order to be able to declaim them effectively and put them to use in the educational programme.

The philosophical studies which form the apex of the higher education of the *Republic's* rulers are echoed in the philosophical studies of Magnesia's Nocturnal Council. Indeed, Plato demands that the members of the Council have some philosophic knowledge, unlike the rest of the citizens. For the latter, education ceases when it has reached the sciences of arithmetic and geometry, somewhere about the twentieth year. On the whole, we are inclined to say that, as in *the Republic*, Plato is still stressing the need for human beings to receive a morally virtuous upbringing and a sound education. He is concerned with the way their souls should be trained in order to follow the virtues of *sophia and phronesis* in particular, and to be properly guided from childhood. The education of the young plays a great part in the moral well-being, *eudaimonia, of* the state.

The Individual and his Freedom

Our aim in this section is to focus attention first on the *Republic* before entering the *Laws*, as both works are concerned with ethics and the individual, politics and the state, and because in both works Plato advocates his notion of freedom that has been held to have totalitarian leanings.

In the plan of the *kallipolis* in the *Republic*, Plato had excluded and abandoned the self-interest of man, his right to own property and to have a family. Now in the *Laws* he includes all the above, and pays particular attention to both family and private property. However, in both works he is always aware of the necessity for limitations on the self-interest of man, so that the latter's individual interests will never become stronger than the public ones, that is, of the state as a whole. This idea of collectivism that Plato is enforcing in both works has offended many who have felt both that his political works, the *Republic* and the *Laws*, express his fondness for absolutism, and that the *Republic* promotes a degree of communism. Above all, both works contain Plato's defence of the view that the state has an interest in the private life and development of the individual and so that there is the need to make complex legal provisions for every aspect of social existence. Hence the claim of many modern philosophers and commentators, most notably Sir Karl Popper, that both works have totalitarian leanings – using a term invented only in the twentieth century.[45]

---

[45] Popper, 1962, 1, p.87.

To start with, what Plato does in the *Republic* is to interpret freedom in the sense that the lower nature should be made to serve the higher one and that equal people should be treated equally and unequal people unequally. For Plato, different social classes should be created to perform different functions, a belief based on the assumption that by nature people have different talents and that as a result they should have different roles within the community.[46] Commentators who have understood the logic of this assumption, they have viewed him as unapologetically non-egalitarian. This is due to his attribution of unlimited powers to the rulers, in the sense that they are not to be constrained by a constitution of laws, whilst the other classes are not even consulted in the decision making or administration and thus have less understanding of their own real interests than the rulers.

In other words, Plato implies that the people who belong to the other two classes can reason, but only to the extent of being intelligent about their own apparent self-interest. Only the guardians can reason in a way that will reflect the interests of all in a way that goes beyond self-interest.[47] Plato thinks that the unity of the state is maintained not by laws and rules but by the guardians' characters and the education that produces this, and that this will involve some manipulation of the ruled by the rulers. Plato here commits himself to a rather undemocratic thesis, to the effect that it would only be the smallest class of the city that would make it well-governed. In the *Republic*, Plato saw freedom as a phenomenon internal to the individual, and not merely as a feature of individuals within society. A man who is master of himself is free as opposed to a man who is a slave of a self that is unfree. The man who is master of himself conducts his life in accordance with those principles which are compatible with what is highest in the human soul, as opposed to the tyrant who is the most unfree of men because he operates in accordance with what is worst in his soul. Therefore, for Plato, freedom operates as a restraint upon a man's particular capacities, withholding him from many things which he has both the desire and the ability to do. Freedom is the internal exercise of control over those parts of one's character which may be considered base, and the establishment of an internal unity of character and personality which enables the complete fulfilment of that which is essentially human. Here Plato divides

---

[46] Plato, *Republic*, 441e.

[47] Ibid., 476a ff. Plato tells us that the philosopher seeks knowledge of the unchanging forms of beauty, justice and so on. Others who content themselves with the particularities of the phenomenal world, that is, with what we can perceive by our senses, do not have the true knowledge of the philosopher but have only belief or opinion based on the mutable appearance of things.

the citizens into classes giving the 'freedom' to the rulers to exercise their control over the masses and 'force' them when necessary to be free.[48] He gave the rulers the power to introduce or remove obstacles which would encourage or prohibit the development of internal freedom. Plato's notion of freedom, therefore, was that true freedom was the freedom of the soul. Freedom for him is not simply to do what one wishes but rather to do the thing which is considered worth doing.

Plato's view may be contrasted with that of a modern political theorist like J.S. Mill,[49] for whom freedom is related to the power of the state as enshrined in law, so that the measure of the freedom of the individual is not the lenience, but the scope of the law that governs him. It is, however, mistaken to approach Plato from the vantage point of Mill, whose *On Liberty* advocates general freedom from interference for all conduct which is 'self-regarding' in not harming directly the important interest of others. Mill recommends that society should neither prohibit not seek to control actions which are only immoral and/or self-harming, for such criteria can never be sufficient justification for restricting freedom.

Although it is an oversimplification, Mill is usually said to understand freedom negatively, as freedom from control. Mill's defence of individual freedom already presupposes the priority of at least a minimal but crucial kind of justice in acknowledging that all mature adults should enjoy the liberty he defends; he recognises the principle of equal rights to freedom and accepts as normal a society in which it is universally available. The radical Sophists with whom Plato was arguing were quite different. They said that justice and equal legal rights were completely indefensible, as Plato's picture of them and their views in his dialogue reveal. For instance, in *Gorgias*,[50] Callicles declares that 'Natural right consists in the better and cleverer man ruling his inferiors and having the lion's share'. Glaucon in the *Republic*[51] emphasises that '...anyone who had the power to do wrong and was a real man would never make any such agreement (to institute justice) – he would be mad if he did'. Thrasymachus in *Republic* I also declares that human beings are naturally acquisitive, competitive, competitive and aggressive, and he admires the tyrant who fleeces his subjects as the shepherd does his sheep. He sees no basis on which the stronger may be criticised if the weaker are foolish enough to be manipulated. Thrasymachus is

---

[48] 'Forcing' people to be free is a phrase that was coined by J.J. Rousseau in his Social Contract, but it could well apply to what Plato was getting at in the *Republic*.
[49] Mill, 1987.
[50] Plato, *Gorgias*, 490a, 492a–c.
[51] Plato, *Republic*, II 359b.

only exposing a general deception by showing that invocations of justice are always nothing but invitations to sacrifice one's self-interest to the stronger who will take advantage.

For those radical Sophists, freedom consists in pursuing one's own advantage successfully – an idea that acknowledges no place for justice and fairness. Thrasymachus puts it most neatly in asserting that injustice given scope has greater strength, freedom and power 'because it rules';[52] it dominates those who are really simple and just while they serve their 'ruler's interests'.[53] From this idea that 'injustice rules', Thrasymachus infers that only the unjust agent with the will and capacity to do as he or she wants is free. Similarly, Glaucon in *Republic II* imagines a supernatural invulnerable invisibility to express the freedom of the unjust person who successfully exploits and controls others for his or her own ends.

Ultimately, for the radical Sophists, freedom means the power to gratify one's appetites and dominate others. So, whereas Mill presupposes certain notions of justice in his principle of liberty, the Sophists challenged Plato to defend even the most minimal claims for equal legal rights.

The second respect in which Plato's perspective on freedom differs radically from Mill's also arises from the Sophists claim that we are free only insofar as we can gratify our appetites, as these are widely understood. Instead of presupposing the legitimacy of rules protecting others interests, and instead of conceiving freedom as the absence of social control external to the agent, Plato adopts an internal approach, and considers human nature to determine whether our freedom is realised only in successful domination of others.

In the *Republic*, having shown that communities may be at once unified and internally diverse, Plato argues that the same is true of human nature, which has three main aspects: reason, spirit and appetite, each of which has different propensities which must be reconciled in any satisfactory life. Because the primary characteristic of humankind is reason, Plato infers that this must rule or guide our lives and that we are only fully human when it does so. In other words, properly understood individual justice is an 'internal' condition in which each aspect of our being achieves its appropriate recognition within our lives.[54] This important idea leads Plato to identify 'real freedom' with the realisation of our true rational selves. Freedom then turns out to be freedom of doing what one wills, and is not the power to satisfy any and every desire

---

[52] Plato, *Republic*, I 344c.
[53] Ibid., I 344c.
[54] Ibid., 443c–e.

but rather to satisfy those desires in which the whole self finds satisfaction. Accordingly, freedom is a phenomenon internal to the individual and not merely a feature of individuals within society: a man who is a master of himself is free as opposed to a man who is a slave of that self. Freedom operates as a restraint upon a man's particular capacities, withholding him from many things which he has the desire and the ability to do. For Plato, freedom implies a realisation of his true, natural self, and what matters for him is neither mere freedom from external control (Mill) or even that combined with the capacity to overcome others (Sophists). Instead, freedom is an internal condition of being free from the domination of appetite and spirit in our natures, in order to realise our rational selves most fully. This condition represents 'true freedom', because it is what all humankind 'really wants'. From this perspective, then, Plato is ready to embrace the seeming paradox that we can be 'forced to be free'.[55] So that it can never be in any man's interest to lose his freedom; only the virtuous man is free; only he is free to achieve what his rational, as opposed to his impulsive, self wants. Plato then acknowledges that if our own rational control is missing 'it must be imposed from without'[56] and so his rulers should not be seen as dictators since they can only do the best for their city. They, in return, have to obey certain unwritten laws; property was to be equally shared out and the sovereigns are neither to own anything nor to have a family. Thus, Plato recommends abolition of the family, communal modes of ownership, and censorship of art and letters, and he holds that all women should be common to all men whilst no parent should know its child.

Of course, according to Plato's notion of collectivism, he was justified in doing whatever he believed was for the good of the commonwealth and was never willing to act against its interests. Because all the citizens have some measure of reason they would understand the need to accept what they are given. It is the same notion of rationality that Plato puts into force in the *Laws*. Here, Plato moves away from his previous 'communist' principles, allowing to each individual a wife, a family and the right to own private property, at least as far as this is necessary to form a household. But each individual is still subordinated to the state of which he is an organic part, and the law, which is described as the dispensation of reason,[57] penetrates into every aspect of life regulating and controlling even domestic functions. The citizens are now

---

[55] See footnote 48.
[56] Plato, *Republic*, 590d.
[57] Plato, *Laws*, 836a.

given more power than in the *kallipolis* due to the existence of the written laws and constitution. Plato still defends the view that the state has an interest in the private life and development of the individual and needs to make complex legal provisions for every aspect of social existence. Hence in both schemes the individual is subordinated to the state. However, it is fair to say that the citizen is now more free both in Plato's and in Mill's sense than in the *kallipolis*, in the sense that he is not left solely to the unfettered discretion of the guardians.

Reason, that has, always been important in Platonic philosophy, is now used by individuals in order to produce the best laws for Magnesia. It is reason that tells them that before they accept any laws they have to understand what the latter are aiming at and what they stand for; thus the idea of the preambles.[58] We may say that the people of Magnesia are becoming important as individuals and that, in general, the *Laws* is a more realistically optimistic work than the *Republic*. In short, what Plato proposes in order to ensure the freedom of the individual and to secure the city both internally and externally will be achieved through law and written legislation. The Athenian is right to assume that the law must be relatively stable, and that it must command the respect of the citizens. Nevertheless, laws can be changed in Magnesia.

As we have noted above, Plato still thinks collectively, and he believes that without collectivism the individual would be nothing at all. He once again emphasises the significance of the group and the collective, advising the Magnesians that they should 'never dream of acting independently and should become utterly incapable of it'. He tells them clearly that Magnesia is the only city in which 'every one lives as much as possible collectively' and that nobody must get into the habit of acting alone and independently.[59] At this point one may object that even though Magnesia is based on law it is still a closed society, as Popper argues in his work *The Open Society and its Enemies*. Popper says that in Magnesia there are restrictions on marriage, making the latter to a great extent compulsory, on military service and so forth. He adds that there is also prohibition of trade and commerce; rigid control of music and the other arts, and a law against atheism. He claims that the city will thus be almost literally a closed society in the sense that foreign contacts will be curtailed and the individual will be deprived of all his freedom as a result of Plato's model of education. Popper[60] should have been more careful and more objective in his critique of Plato's notion of foreign contacts and importing goods, for, if we

---

[58] Plato, *Laws*, 722b–723a.
[59] Ibid., 942c.
[60] Popper, 1962. Popper thinks that it is almost a closed society in the sense that foreign contacts will be curtailed as far as possible. See also Plato, *Laws*, 704d–705b, 950d–953e.

examine Plato closely, his prohibition of trade could well be justified, at least from his own point of view. In the same way, he could also be justified in his law against atheism: he believes that people ought to have faith in God or Gods as he feels that without faith and hope, life would be meaningless.

Modern western societies put more power of censorship in the hands of parents and less in the hands of the state. A Platonic authoritarianism and censorship in education may not now be in force in Britain even with the National Curriculum, but in some other societies censorship is still evident due to the notion of collectivism that, at least in theory, is adopted. As such, I believe that Popper's perspective is countered to the extent that censorship, whether in the hands of parents or in the hands of the state, can be found in many western societies. It may sound as if I am defending Plato here, and indeed I do believe that there is more to be said in Plato's favour than in the favour of many western liberals. This includes Plato's treatment of women and their freedom in the states he constructed both in the *Republic* and the *Laws*, considering the role of women in Athenian society in general. This topic is discussed in the following section.

Women in Classical Attica and their Images in Literature

The role, private lives and social position of women in classical antiquity have been the subject of speculation by many commentators whose contribution I freely acknowledge; I ought to give them credit as they have all shed light on the subject in far greater depth than my purposes will allow me to do here. Nevertheless, I shall attempt to explore the same territory, 'rather inaccessible' to historical record, as accurately and incisively as I can. I say 'rather inaccessible', as the knowledge we have about the social role, thoughts and private lives of women in classical antiquity comes largely from literature written by men. What adds to the difficulty of assessing the function of women is that they are portrayed differently by different people, so we ought to be very cautious in our treatment of the views expressed by tragedians, historians, biographers and orators of the time. However, if we do consider representatives of all the above arts, we may come to a more balanced and less shortsighted view than those offered by scholars like A.W. Gomme[61] and W.K. Lacey[62] some time ago, which would be said to be 'old-fashioned' examples of research on women. Gomme bases his account almost exclusively on the evidence from classical tragedy, and expresses the belief that the heroines of

---

[61] Gomme, pp.1–25.
[62] Lacey, 1968.

the latter were modelled directly on Athenian women of the fifth century. Lacey, in contrast to Gomme, places all his emphasis upon the Attic orators, who are hardly included in Gomme's evidence. Both hesitate to rely on comedy. It is hard to evaluate the accuracy of their accounts, and even harder to judge whether women in Athens really had such strong personalities, as the tragedians portray them as having, or if their function was mostly limited to the domestic sphere as the historians claim.

On the whole, even though it might sound a mere oversimplification, it is fair to say that women in ancient Athens had less freedom than in the Dorian states. Their main function was to ensure the smooth operation of the household, that is, the preparation and presentation of food and the safe birth and careful upbringing of their children for whose sake their husbands valued them. However, women in ancient Attic tragedies were presented as fully developed personalities, which makes us wonder at the apparent contradiction when from other sources we learn that women could neither decide for themselves nor plan their lives with a reasonable degree of certainty.

In Euripides' *The Trojan Women*[63] we hear Andromache say, 'I stayed at home. And indoors I didn't practise fancy speech like many women. My mind sound by nature was my teacher. I needed no whore. I offered my husband a silent tongue and gentle looks. I knew when to have my way and when to let him have his.'

In Sophocles' *Antigone*[64] Ismene, her sister, tells Antigone '...we were born women showing that we were not meant to fight with men', implying that it is by nature rather than by man-made convention that women do not attempt to rival men.

Aristophanes' *Ecclesiazusae*[65] Praxagora, disguised as a man, rehearsing a speech which she will give in the assembly in which she says, 'I will demonstrate that they are all our superiors. First one and all, they colour their wool in boiling dyes in the traditional way; you'd never find them changing. If we'd stuck loyally to this, instead of chasing after novelties wouldn't our country have been saved. They sit down to cook, as in days gone by; they carry bundles on their heads as in days gone by; they celebrate Demeter's mysteries as in days gone by; they bake their cakes as in days gone by, they hug their husbands as in days gone by; they receive their lovers as in days gone by; they buy

---

[63] Euripides, *The Trojan Women*, 642–51.
[64] Sophocles, *Antigone*, 61–69.
[65] Aristophanes, *Ecclesiazusae*, 214–228.

goodies on the sly, as in days gone by; they adore pure wine, as in days gone by; they enjoy sex as in days gone by'.

We need to note at this point that even though this speech is made for comic purposes, it nevertheless includes some comments against women.

In Aristophanes' *Lysistrata*[66] we also hear how difficult the women find it to get a meeting: 'Oh my dear, they'll come. It's not easy for women to get away. We're always dancing attendance on our husbands, or getting the maid moving, or putting the baby to bed, bathing it, feeding it'.

Yet Xenophon, in *Oeconomicus*,[67] tells us that women's work was mainly productive, having a lot of similarities with that of the slaves, but that a number of women would help their husbands and would have a partnership with them, if the latter had previously taught them their art. And Xenophon describes the wife who masters the science of economics as having a 'masculine mind'. I interpret this as an intention to imply merely that while it was not natural for a woman to master the science of economics, it could be done.

Aristotle, too, in his *Politics*,[68] argued that it was considered natural for a husband to rule over his wife and children. He deduced that the friendship between husband and wife was 'unequal' and that the connubial relationship was based on utility, in contrast to the equitable relationships between men which are the basis of social and political organisation. Man and wife need each other, Aristotle admitted, but their relationship was between benefactor and beneficiary. Aristotle was describing the patriarchal family of classical Athens, but his influence was widespread and enduring.

Plutarch[69] tells us that any husband ought to show affection to a good wife three times a month because the result will be a reduction in marital tensions. Xenophon[70] tells us that the husband is obliged to sleep three times a month with his wife and then he was free to enjoy the company of his fellows in homosexual relations or to consort with prostitutes. Thus, married Athenian men were allowed to copulate with prostitutes; a great number of these were slaves and could be passed on to friends of their master.

---

[66] Aristophanes, *Lysistrata*, 15–9.
[67] Xenophon, *Oeconomicus*, VII 10–14, 22, 30.
[68] Aristotle, *Politics*, 1.2.12 1254b, 15 1239 60; Aristotle, *Eudemian Ethics*, 7.10 (8–9) 1272a, 7.3.3 (1283b), 7/5/5 (1239b).
[69] Plutarch, *Solon*, 20.3.
[70] Xenophon, *Oeconomicus*, III 10–11, VII 10–14, 22, 30.

Even though Herodotus[71] says that the Egyptians, 'like the Greeks', each had only one wife – that is, that both the Greeks and the Egyptians were monogamous – they were nevertheless allowed to enjoy the company of *hetairai* (courtesans) and prostitutes or whores *(pornai)*, and that of young boys, whereas for women we have no evidence of similar behaviour.

However, in the *Ecclesiazusae*, we hear that Praxagora, being married to an old man, has difficulty in satisfying her sexual needs. One part of the reform she demands is that a beautiful young man can be forced into intercourse with her. Women in general were required to get married young, and I believe it was justifiable for a young girl to get married to someone twice her age as Xenophon tells us in *Oeconomicus;* Plato in the *Republic* suggested females should become parents for the first time at twenty and males at thirty. Later on, in the *Laws*,[72] Plato reduced the minimum age for females to any time between sixteen and twenty. Both life expectancy and the length of time during which one can have children are very relevant here: quite a lot of women died in childbirth, and women cannot bear children after the menopause, whereas men can go on begetting them.

In spite of the fact that the position of women, as described so far, was mainly in the domestic sphere, many plots of tragedy, derived from myths of the Bronze Age preserved mainly by the Homeric epics, presented their heroines with strong personalities unlike those of the Athenian women. Although this seems to be a contradiction at first sight, it becomes clear why the tragedians of the time portrayed them in that way if we understand the origin of these myths. The royal women of the *Iliad* and *the Odyssey* were indeed powerful, not simply within their household, but even in the external political sense. One needs to remember that the age when these poems were written was characterised by the existence of matriarchy which was later replaced by patriarchy. [Of course this, it needs to be said, is a theory and not a fact.]

However, in deriving their plots from the epic poems, the tragedians could not completely ignore the epic portrayal of women. In some cases, like that of Clytemnestra in the *Oresteia*,[73] Aeschylus portrays her as murdering her husband and thus makes her more powerful than she was portrayed originally in Homer, where it is implied that it was her lover rather than Clytemnestra herself who killed her husband. Of course, this point about Clytemnestra

---

[71] Herodotus, 2.92.
[72] Plato, *Laws*, VII 833d.
[73] Aeschylus, *The Oresteia*.

might seem to destroy the claim that tragedy inherits its powerful women from Homer but we also have other examples of such women. In Euripides' Medea,[74] for example, we see Medea murder her sons and take revenge on her unfaithful husband, while in Sophocles' *Antigone*[75] we see Antigone take credit for an act of civil disobedience. I am inclined to believe that one should not accept that the actions of these women had something in common with Athenian women generally. It may be possible to view these images of women in tragedy as images serving the purpose of a tragedian. However, this purpose could vary and so one should not rely solely on tragedy for one's research on women, as Gomme has done. But it would be equally wrong to rely too heavily upon Attic orators' as Lacey has done, though I appreciate his rejection of tragedy as not being representative of normal people in a normal family. What seems to me a more plausible picture of the fifth and fourth centuries BC is what Demosthenes tells us: 'we have *hetairai* for pleasure, concubines for our day-to-day physical well-being, and wives in order to beget legitimate children, and have trustworthy guardians of our households'.

Although Dover[76] insists that we cannot consider this the definitive fourth century view, I feel that it contains at least some truth, though I am aware that it was also written by a man.

Equality of Education as a Sufficient Factor in the Equality of the Sexes

My aim in this section is to focus attention on some additional aspects of the *Republic's* educational theory, as for Plato equal education implies equality of the sexes. When Plato talks about the community of men and women, he argues that both sexes should be able to perform the same duties according to their natural ability, ignoring completely their biological differences. He thus makes women, as a class, equal to men, as far as their capacities are concerned, but, on the whole, weaker in all pursuits, arguing that men will generally perform better than women. What is particularly important in this dialogue is his notion that women are to be trained and educated in exactly the same way as men.

Women who are of philosophical dispositions will become guardians too, as in Book V[77] where we hear that both male and female sheep dogs are

---

[74] Euripides, *Medea*.
[75] Sophocles, *Antigone*.
[76] Dover, 1978.
[77] Plato, *Republic*, V 449c–473e.

equally responsible for guarding the flock. Both female and male rulers will guard the city, protecting it in war and ruling it in peace. Socrates immediately corrects Glaucon who thought that in the ideal state there would be ruling men who could be morally good and noble, telling him:

> And ruling women too, Glaucon I said. Don't suppose that what I have said applies any more to men than to women, all those who are born among them with adequate natures. There is no practice of a city's governors which belongs to woman because she's woman or to man because he's man, but the natures are scattered alike among both animals and woman participates according to nature in all practices, and man in all, but in all of them women is 'weaker than man'.[78]

By this, Plato means that women may be equal to men in nature and yet inferior in capacity because of physiological differences which are likely to make them end up at an inferior level to men if required to perform the same tasks. However, in spite of their weaknesses and the fact that he thinks that women are more cowardly, less trustworthy and innately worse than men, he nevertheless argues for their equal training with men in gymnastics and music.

Here, it must be noted that Plato intended to offer the same practices in preparation for ruling to both men and women, in order to do what he felt was according to nature. He understands that what is natural is to offer equal opportunities to both sexes so that women should participate in the same gymnastic training as men in order to ensure they gain the necessary physical strength and discipline in order to be guardians. Male and female guardians must not be allowed to live together in the same household, and should not be allowed to own any property. In other words, he applies a form of communism with equality of the sexes and the abolition of both private property and the family. In fact, it is these principles that Leo Strauss thinks 'are against nature' and will present Plato's just city from coming into being, so that his Utopia is an unrealisable plan.[79]

Plato then moves on to say that all women should be common to all men, and that children should be held in common, to be brought up in state nurseries. No parent should know its child and vice versa. Thus, with the abolition of the family, women in the *Republic* are moved away from the habitual sphere and are not required to love and care for their children and be

---

[78] Plato, *Republic*, 454e.
[79] Strauss, 1977.

restricted solely to the domestic context. They are now given the opportunity to play the same leadership role as men in society. However, commentators throughout the subsequent centuries have often been offended by this point, possibly because the majority of them were men. Barker[80] feels that this Platonic proposal for the equality of the sexes is unnatural because what is natural for women is a lifetime of motherhood. So, what Plato says indeed 'makes her able to inspire noble enthusiasm, but not to direct a policy or drill a regiment as Plato would require his mother–ruler as woman soldiers to do'.

Barker's suggestion reminds us of Aristotle, for whom 'the male is by nature superior and the female inferior and the one ruler and the other ruled'.[81] For Plato, both man and woman alike who will be true philosophers, reaching knowledge of the good through reason and dialectic, should be called philosopher–kings.[82] This seems for many commentators, mostly feminists, a paradox, as Plato does not mention the concept of 'philosopher–queens' as the latter would have expected him to have done. They therefore think that he is either intending to make women like men or that he is not an actual believer in the equality of the sexes because 'he could not or did not wish to free himself from the Athenian prejudice which treated women legally as perpetual minors' as the classicist and feminist Sarah Pomeroy holds.[83] However, I believe that Pomeroy should have offered better and stronger evidence in order to make her position more tenable, because as it stands it is not totally convincing.

Popper too, it must be noted, does not consider the issue important enough to discuss, and ignores Plato's advocacy of women rulers, believing that women at the time were viewed as property, but he nevertheless argues for Plato's totalitarianism whilst criticising Plato's feminism.

Another position which I find very unattractive is that of Allan Bloom,[84] who holds that when Plato includes women in the guardian class he does so because of his awareness of their reproductive function and not because he genuinely entertains the possibility of their having the same natures as men. This position is unconvincing, because there would be enough women in the ideal state for the reproductive function without making some women guardians. Yet after the 1960s, with the advent of a new feminist movement and the entry of more women into philosophy, there have been many who have emphasised Plato's misogyny. It is true that in the *Republic* Plato describes

---

[80] Barker, 1959, p.148; Barker, 1947, p.vi; Jaeger, 1943, vol. II, p.244.
[81] Aristotle, *Politics*, 1259a 37–1259b 17.
[82] Plato, *Republic*, 473d.
[83] Pomeroy, 1975, pp.115–19.
[84] Bloom, 1968.

a woman's mind as small, and says that 'imitating a woman' in sexual encounters, that is, assuming the submissive position, is humiliating.[85] In the *Timeaus*[86] myth, to exist as a woman is to be in an inferior state. Nevertheless, it is equally true that Plato attempted to involve women in politics, an area traditionally under male domination and control. Whether he did this because *the Republic* was meant to be a Utopia, and he therefore needed to put forward very radical proposals, or because it meant what he prescribed, and he would have really like to see the involvement of women in politics, is not something of which we have conclusive knowledge.

Similarly, we have no knowledge of whether Plato was responding to Aristophanes' *Ecclesiazusae (Women in Parliament)*. What we do know is what we can read in the dialogue itself, and I believe that if many feminists had paid reasonable attention to Plato's proposals of equality in the fourth century, they would not have been offended by the fact that he felt that women should have the chance to see if they could measure up to male achievement. There is nothing wrong with this idea, as the world in which he was living was under male domination and it was generally believed that women were made by nature to perform jobs such as giving birth to children, caring for them and bringing them up, jobs that men would fail in doing. Plato disqualifies this position and gives women more fights than they ever had before. Respected and knowledgeable commentators such as Julia Annas ought to be more satisfied with Plato's proposals, and should neither be concerned with some inconsistencies they might find in his account nor spend time in deciding what he should have said or explaining what they would wish him to have said.

The commentators who have emphasised the fact that Plato is not a forerunner of women's liberation are quite unreasonable. Annas[87] says that Plato is not concerned with the women guardians' desires and needs, but couldn't she understand that what Plato said was that because they were to become guardians they ought to have the same restrictions on child rearing applied to men also equally?

Certainly, she may argue that Plato is authoritarian, but to say that women should have some monopoly on ability in some areas is no more than a feminist principle of our own time. Does Plato say that men would have some monopoly on ability in some areas? No, but what he definitely thinks is that

---

[85] Plato, *Republic*, 395c–397c.
[86] Plato, *Timeaus*, 42b–c.
[87] Annas, 1981, p.181–5.

equality in education would contribute to the equality of the sexes. Although the majority of the feminists have argued against this view, I nevertheless sympathise with Plato, as he truly intends to offer equal opportunities to the two sexes. If people are born with different innate talents, and it happens that more women than men are better fitted for the task of ruling, or vice versa, he does not offer any objection. He feels that anyone who becomes ruler should be educated and trained equally before he or she is given the task.

Women in the *Laws*

In the *Republic*, it is true to say that Plato abolishes women's traditional sphere, as he defends the value of sexual communism and thus makes women common to all men. In the *Laws*, he defends monogamy and private households, and reinstates the family, reallocating women to nurturing and to tasks concerned with children. What are we to make out of these apparently different Platonic views on women? Does the *Laws* contradict what Plato had previously expressed in the *Republic* about women? Or is the *Laws* in total agreement with Plato's views on women in the earlier work, and are we to take them both as two components of a single, unified, consistent view? The aim of this section will be to show how Plato's views on the subject can be legitimately accepted and consistent though I appreciate that a 'devil's advocate' might say that the move back to individual families in the *Laws* is so fundamental that my claim for consistency rings rather hollow. Nevertheless, in order to stress the consistency of the works on the whole as far as women are concerned I hope to make it clear by examining the *Laws* closely.

In the *Laws* Plato is clearly thinking of the Greek family, and, being a Greek, he speaks like one who above all values the idea of collectivism, considering the latter as the main contributor to *eudaimonia* – the *eudaimonia* of the state as a whole rather than of any isolated individuals. In considering women, Plato is primarily interested in putting them in the most appropriate place in order to function harmoniously with the rest of society.

Although in the *Republic*[88] he appears to give women the opportunity to measure up to male function and achievement, arguing that women and men have identical natures, in the *Laws* he acknowledges their biological differences. While in the former he argues that both sexes should be equally trained in gymnastics and music in preparation for ruling, in the *Laws*,[89] he considers specific natural differences between the physical nature of men and women

---

[88] Plato, *Republic*, 451d ff.
[89] Plato, *Laws*, 794c–d, 796a ff., 802a ff., 805a ff.–806b.

and proposes that they should be taught different words and music. Even though the point raised above seems a contradiction of the *Republic*, it is fair to say that Plato, understanding the differences between men and women, which is a point denied in the *Republic*, stresses that there should be some basis for discrimination between the two sexes. If considered thoroughly, this seeming inconsistency is no more than a correction Plato must have felt he needed to make in order to make his argument more coherent and more in accord with Magnesia, which is not a Utopia, but a society designed to be an actual realisable plan.

In thinking about women, Plato, as in the *Republic*, still regards them as equal to men in capacity, although on the whole weaker in all pursuits. As in the *Republic*, he puts forward strong declarations that women are capable of pursing the same tasks as men so that both in their political function and their military services they are equal to men. Being by nature different from men, Plato thinks in the *Laws* that women's military strength in the protection of the state should be limited to times when the men's army is fighting outside the state. This point is in total agreement with the *Republic*, where Plato also makes it clear that men are able to do anything but describes women as weaker than men, and portrays them as having small minds.[90] This is because he believes that men are more positive, violent and argumentative than women, who are portrayed as more cowardly, less trustworthy, and innately lesser. It is true that the same spirit exists in the *Laws*, where he describes women as secretive, crafty and less capable of virtue than men, and portrays them as naturally inferior to men because of their weakness.[91]

It is fair to say that although the general attitude is the same in the *Republic*, Plato puts women in positions that they actually had in Greek society. He now respects the individual freedom of women more, as he does not make them common to all men. I feel this development would have pleased Annas[92] who argues that Plato in the *Republic* deprives women of their freedom as he abolishes the family and property and defends the ideal of sexual communism.

Here, in the *Laws*, Plato no longer allows this koinobitic principle to be enacted in the ideal state. In contrast he makes marriage between men and women compulsory in that men must get married between thirty and thirty-five and presumably stay married after thirty-five. For women this obligation begins from their sixteenth year, and they are to give birth to healthy children.

---

[90] Plato, *Republic*, 454e: 'weaker than men'; 469d 'small womanish mind'.
[91] Plato, *Laws*, 780e–781b.
[92] Annas, p.181 ff.

One of their duties, as in the *Republic*, is that whilst pregnant they ought to exercise daily.[93] Aristotle[94] also suggests that pregnant women should be forced to exercise by means of a law that they must take daily walks to worship the divinities presiding over childbirth. He believes that the optimum age for marriage was eighteen for women, and thirty-seven for men.

What the *Republic* and the *Laws* do have in common is compulsory common meals. Plato now thinks that if women attend the same common meals as the men, they will have less rigorous attendance requirements and thereby risk becoming second class citizens. Besides, if common meals prompt homosexual misconduct, the mixing of men and women threatens to prompt heterosexual misconduct to an even greater extent. Plato thinks that there must be separate tables, and that if the women are to attend their own tables, regularly they must be allowed to bring little children. Thus, Plato is still keen on the common tables though with some modifications. For example, he understands that the position of the tables can be near one another so that women will cooperate in their public duties.[95] This Platonic intention to separate the women from men is in no way an anti-female expressing Plato's misogyny, as some have claimed, but is Plato's attempt to protect women. To put it in his own words, Plato tells us that '...for example these physical exercises and common meals you speak of, though in many ways beneficial to a city provide dangerous openings for *factio* as is shown by the cases of the Milesians, Boeotians and Thurians, And in particular this practise is generally held to have corrupted the ancient and natural rule in the matter of sexual indulgence common to mankind...' He goes on to say '...we must not forget that this pleasure is held to have been granted by nature to male and female, when conjoined for the work of procreation. The crime of male with male and female with female is an outrage on nature and capita surrender to lust for pleasure. And you know it is our universal accusation against the Cretans that they were the inventors of the tale of Ganymede'.[96]

Aristotle, too, in his *Politics*[97] tells us that for the Cretans, intercourse with males was treated as a practice to prevent overpopulation. He tells us that '...the legislation of Crete contains a number of ingenious devices intended to encourage an abstemious form of diet in the interest of the state; it also includes a provision for the segregation of women, to prevent them from

---

[93] Plato, *Republic*, V 452, 460e; Plato, *Laws*, VI 785, VIII 833d.
[94] Aristotle, *Politics*, VII 14.4, 14.9 (1335a–b).
[95] Plato, *Laws*, 806c.
[96] Ibid., 636.
[97] Ibid., 646.

having too many children and it sanctions homosexual connections'. Plato in the passage quoted above counts it a crime for female to be in love with another female for pleasure. We may wonder how this view relates to the actual behaviour of classical Greek women. Unfortunately, there is not enough evidence available for us to treat female homosexuality in ancient Greece with precision and accuracy. The strongest evidence for female homosexuality we have is to be found in the poetry of Sappho, but even this presents problems of interpretation.

Male Homosexuality

In this section, we are aiming to focus our attention on the way the ancient Greeks viewed male homosexuality in order better to understand why Plato condemns homosexual love in the *Laws*. It is true that the way in which the Greeks viewed homosexuality varies a good deal from our own. This in part has to do with our Christian notions of sex and homosexuality. In Christianity, sex is a sin, and is only for the purpose of procreation. Homosexual sex is seen as an even worse sin, as it is unnatural. In ancient times, however, Greek ideas of homosexuality were formed from some of the Greeks' perceptions. First is that of beauty, which was regularly associated with Eros. Second, comes the conception that true and genuine love could only be found in a relationship between men whilst heterosexual love was regarded as being of low quality, as women in general were thought to be inferior to men. Third, they made an association between education and homosexuality.

Homer, in Book VI of the *Odyssey*[98] tells us that when Odysseus had been washed up in the land of the Phaeacians and was faced by the princess Nausicaa whom he wished to win over to help him, he compared her with Artemis and said, 'You are more beautiful than any woman or man that I have ever seen.' Coming from the much travelled Odysseus, this is indeed a great compliment. However, to the modern ear it does sound slightly odd that Nausicaa is compared with men as well as women.

The Greeks saw beauty as a thing that young men should strive for as well as young girls. Homosexual relationships were, on the whole, tolerated in Greek society. This was partly because they served a basic utilitarian purpose: a man could marry and have children and yet still conduct a homosexual relationship. In fact it was *better* that it was a homosexual relationship, as there was no jealousy for his wife, no worry of illegitimate children making claims on his land, and, above all, he received sexual gratification. In this way, the

---

[98] Homer, *Odyssey*, VI.

role of young boys became equivalent to the role of mistresses. Naturally, there would be fights between two men over the affections of the same boy. The law, however, protected males from rape as well as women.

Young boys and women were considered as weak as each other in sexual matters. In the Archaic period, Theognis says that boys and women are ready to love 'the man at hand'.[99] This makes them rather more like vessels or objects of love, not capable of love themselves, although the younger boys become able with age.

By the classical period, homosexuality had become a normal part of Greek life. In Aristophanes' *Clouds*[100] we hear, 'Just consider my young friend, everything that's involved in being 'good' and all the pleasures you're going to miss: boys, women... good food, laughs'.

Xenophon, in his *Memorabilia*[101] defines vice as 'advising a man to have sex with a boy and virtue as not treating a boy like a woman'. The ancient Greeks saw it also as quite natural that education and homosexuality could go hand in hand. Most relationships in classical times involved an older man and a younger boy, and the most natural of these was between teacher and pupil. More precisely, the ancient Greeks did not speak of what we now term homosexuality but they talked about *paiderastias schesis*, (παιδεραστίας σχέσις) that is, a relationship of someone of the age twelve and eighteen with an older man. They rarely even spoke of a relationship between two men of the same age.

Even though we do not actually know if much of what we now regard as historical evidence contains an objective picture of the ancient world, we may say that from the age of twelve and until they reached the age of eighteen, boys were regarded as justified in having erotic friendships with others of the same sex. Although Dover[102] makes a full treatment of the question of paederasty using material from both literature and archaeology, I believe that he does not critically consider the latter.

This friendship between men was a phenomenon socially acceptable in ancient Greece and was based on some rules which if not observed properly led to punishment. However, from the time that the young boy was starting 'to have a beard', that is, he was starting to become an adult, he was no longer *eromenos*.[103] This was a general Greek custom whose purpose was to help

---

[99] Theognis, II – CF.M.L. West (43–5).
[100] Aristophanes, *Clouds*.
[101] Xenophon, *Memorabilia*.
[102] Dover, 1978.
[103] Plato, *Protagoras*, 309a.

young boys change themselves in time and gradually become perfect men. Accordingly, any violence involved in such a relationship could make their *eros para physin* (unnatural) and was viewed as *hybris*. In that way, the *hybristes* was punished by losing his political rights.

To bribe a young boy in order to perform sexual intercourse with his friend was considered to be *hybris*, too. The young boy could only offer himself to his friend without money, for the sake of their friendship, although such friendship could include presents. However, to perform feminine functions was prohibited and whatever was regarded as natural for women's sexual actions was unnatural for the young boy.

Paiderasty, according to, A. Patzer,[104] ought to be examined as a cultural phenomenon and be judged in itself and in its time without our present tendency to compare it with present views. According to this view, Greek paederasty has two types: the Dorian type that was concerned with *arete* in war, and the classical that aimed at helping the future of the citizens. In the first case, the erotic action was not concerned with bodily pleasure but with a social task. Through sexual actions, the *erastes* was communicating with his *eromenos*, *the arete* required of the latter at this time until he became an adult.

In the classical type, the basic rule is *o dikaios eros* (just love), a just relationship. Among other *aretai*, the lovers appreciate being *kalos k'agathos* (fine and noble) as a reflection of one's internal character. The intimate relationship of *kaloi kagathoi* (fine and noble) lovers was accepted, in Athens at least, as it was thought to contribute to the 'building of a bridge' between generations.

Xenophon[105] tells us that whilst *paiderasty* was accepted in Athens, homosexuality was heavily criticised in Sparta. The explanation is that in Sparta the *syssitia*, and generally the whole organisation of the state, divided the generations. There were conflicts over finance and authority between father and son. S.C. Humphreys[106] remarks that in the absence of trust between fathers and sons, it was natural that the sons would trust an *erastes* who would promise to help them with their education until they became adults and would perform the role of a father figure to them. In Plato's dialogues and in the works of Plutarch, Lucian and Aristophanes amongst others, there are allusions to homosexual relationships. However, these allusions do not necessary imply either the authors' homosexuality or their acceptance of the latter. Moreover, I do not believe that the mention of ancient myths such as that of Zeus and

---

[104] Patzer, 1966.
[105] Xenophon, *Constitution of the Lacedaemonians*, B13.
[106] Humphreys, 1915.

Ganymede or that of Laios and Chrysippus implies the acceptance of the sexual practices in these myths. On the contrary, I would argue that the mention of such myths could well be meant to imply the disastrous consequences of such behaviour or merely to emphasise the fact that people in general did not live in this way.

To be more precise about Plato, in the *Symposium*[107] he puts a tale into the mouth of Alcibiades in order to illustrate Socrates' relationship with the young Alcibiades. What it is worth saying here is that Plato, when discussing homosexuality, means homosexuality between men and men rather than women and women. We also need to note that, according to the *Symposium*, the relationship between Socrates and Alcibiades was not a physical one, in spite of Alcibiades' wish for such a relationship. Socrates here, probably speaking for Plato, is evidently against the physical consummation of such relationships. Nevertheless, he understands that each side could gain from a relationship between an *erastes* and an *eromenos*. The older man would receive sexual gratification while the young boy would gain wisdom and experience from the older man. This being the case, it would be in the interest of young boys to become involved with older men of note, as the results would be beneficial to them. However, it was viewed as scandalous when a young boy, like Alcibiades in the *Symposium*, attempted to take the initiative in his relations with Socrates, trying to trick the latter into bed with him. Nevertheless, what is particularly striking in the *Symposium* is that Plato, whilst discussing the notion of *eros*, tells us that in homosexual relationships there is a more intense *eros* that in heterosexual ones. The *Symposium* is not the only one in which Plato alludes to homosexuality, though it is the only dialogue in which he discusses the nature of homosexual love. In *Protagoras*[108] the unnamed friend who meets Socrates at the opening of their dialogue asks him where he comes from: 'Where have you come from Socrates? Well, I suppose it's obvious from chasing around after Alcibiades' beauty', making a second mention in Plato's dialogues of Socrates' presumed homosexual relationship with Alcibiades.

In other dialogues, Plato alludes to the *erastes* of Parmenides, Zeno;[109] to Meno's *erastes*, Aristippos;[110] to Hippothales and Lysis;[111] to Ktesipppos and Kleinias.[112] It is in the last of these that Socrates says they there is nothing

---

[107] Plato, *Symposium*, 216–219e.
[108] Plato, *Protagoras*, 309a.
[109] Plato, *Parmenides*, 127b.
[110] Plato, *Meno*, 70b.
[111] Plato, *Lysis*, 205–206.
[112] Plato, *Euthydemus*, 282b.

disgraceful or objectionable in subordination or enslavement to an *erastes* to or any person in complete readiness to perform any of those services which are honourable and out of zeal for becoming wise.

In the *Republic*[113] Plato sees *eros* as a problem for justice, believing that if man were not erotic and did not let his desires rule over his reason, there would be no need for justice. He tells us that 'right *eros*' in the ideal state permits the *erastes* to touch his *paidika* as 'a son' but to go no further than that. Plato here aims to tame man's erotic nature, civilising him and making him moderate and disciplined in the interests of internal peace and order.

Phaedrus[114] in a speech alleged to be by Lysias, and or perhaps a parody of Lysias, though Plato is in no way committed to what is said there, it presumably tells us something about the prevailing attitudes of his time. One of the latter was that against physical homosexual relationships. However, this is not to say that Plato did not understand that homosexuality was indeed a social phenomenon in his time.

In the *Laws*[115] Plato harshly rejects sexual relationships between men, regarding these as *para physin*. He mentions an old law that Laios did not obey and which brought the ensuing results. He also uses the term *ataktos Aphrodite* (disorderly Aphrodite)[116] in order to stress the unnaturalness of such love. Here we must stress that the use of *nomimos* (lawful) in ancient Greece could imply what was *kata physin* as regards the sexual relationships of both men and women. According to an inscription of Lindos,[117] *nomimon* was what was according to *physis* whilst in another inscription of Lindos[118] the sexual relationships that were *para* were para *nomous*. And it is indeed the *para physin* relationships that Plato attacks in the *Laws*. He puts forward proposals that would condemn the consummation of homosexual desire and love on the grounds that they were contrary to nature. In the *Laws*, for the first time, Plato, despite understanding that by nature everyone is led towards people who are like one's self, more explicitly and more clearly related to the psychological theory of the *Republic*, condemns the consummation of homosexual desire and love.'[119] In doing so he deals once again with the old distinction between *physis and nomos*, between nature and social convention. However, his

---

[113] Plato, *Republic*, 403b.
[114] Plato, *Phaedrus*, 231e.
[115] Plato, *Laws*, 636, 835–841.
[116] Plato, *Laws*, 840e.
[117] IG xiii, 789, 4.
[118] XIII, 487, 19.
[119] Plato, *Laws*, 840.

condemnation of homosexuality is not as provocative as it might appear at first glance; it is simply a restatement of his view of man's ability to resist temptation to bodily pleasure. Indeed, this idea is fully in accord with the moral tradition of the time and with his own philosophy as expressed in the *Republic* in particular.

In the *Laws*[120] Plato declares that 'homosexual intercourse and lesbianism seem to be unnatural crimes of the first rank, and are committed because men and women cannot control their desire for pleasure'. For Plato, the pleasure of heterosexual intercourse is granted in accordance with nature whereas homosexual pleasure is 'contrary to nature' and a 'crime' caused by the failure to control the desire for pleasure, and he finds that both Crete and Sparta, were examples of such a phenomenon. He criticises the legislation in force in both Crete and Sparta where homosexuality was supposed to flourish more than in Athens. His criticism does not mean that homosexuality did not exist in Athens, only that it was less evident there.

We now need to focus our attention on Plato's attempt to find a way to establish what is natural and what is not.

His prohibition of homosexual relations was due to his idea that they go beyond what nature shows to be adequate in sexual pleasure. Plato had already paid attention to the control of unnatural desires in his theory of the tripartite soul and the allegory of the cave in the *Republic*. There, Plato shows us that desires should obey reason. I am inclined to think that in the *Laws* Plato is putting this idea into practice, as he shows us that desires for homosexual intercourse are simply an indication of an insufficiently disciplined soul. Such a soul, being blind, desires homosexual copulation among other pleasurable sensations. In this way, Plato thinks these people cannot frame a moral code for themselves, due to their ignorance of what is natural, just like those in the cave who are equally ignorant because of their lack of knowledge of the form of the good. But does Plato in both works succeed in showing that psychologically well-balanced people do what is natural and can be prevented from having such desires? Certainly, Plato knows that people have desires and emotions and he is not trying to prevent them. What he aims at doing is to help them to control their desires and emotions in order to achieve their moral potential in life. In order to do that, the appetitive element of the soul has to obey reason, so that by reasoning we shall learn what is natural and what is not. But the term 'nature' of course is an ambiguous one, and, so, one might easily disagree with Plato's argument about homosexuality being

---

[120] Plato, *Laws*, 636c.

'contrary to nature'. Plato, in condemning homosexuality, should have given us stronger evidence, or he should have explicitly drawn the distinction Aristotle drew in the *Nicomachean Ethics*.[121] Aristotle distinguishes what is naturally pleasurable from what is pleasurable without being naturally so, but all Plato does here is to argue that one should control even 'the strongest desires':[122]

> Anyone who, in conformity with nature proposes to re-establish the law as it was before Laios (the mythical inventor of homosexuality), declaring that it was right not to join with men and boys in sexual intercourse as with females adducing as evidence the nature of animals and pointing out that male does not touch male for sexual purposes, since that is not natural, he could I think make a very strong case.

No one, continues the Athenian, could argue that the law should take a benevolent view of homosexual relations, for these do not implant courage in the soul of the 'persuaded' or self-restraint in the 'persuader'; the latter is open to blame as failing to withstand the temptations of pleasure and the former as 'mimicking the female'.[123] The Athenian's proposal is that the religious sanctions which already operate against incest, so that 'not so much as a desire for such intercourse enters most people's heads',[124] should be extended to sexual legislation in general:[125]

> That is precisely what I meant in saying that I had an idea for reinforcing the law about the natural use of the intercourse which procreates children abstaining from the male not deliberately killing human progeny or 'sowing in rocks and stones', where it will never take root and be endowed with growth abstaining too from all female soil in which you would not want what you have sown to grow. This law... confers innumerable benefits. In the first place it has been made according to nature, also it debars men from erotic fury and insanity from all kinds of adultery and all excesses in drink and food, and it makes men truly affectionate to their own wives.

---

[121] Aristotle, *Nicomachean Ethics*, 1148b 15–19–20.
[122] Plato, *Laws*, 836d–e.
[123] Ibid., 846a–c.
[124] Ibid., 838b.
[125] Ibid., 838, 839b.

What Plato tells us here is a restatement or further development of what he has told us earlier in the dialogue:[126]

> Our citizens should not be inferior to birds and many other species of animals which are born in large communities and up to the age of procreation live unmated, pure and unpolluted by marriage, but when they have arrived at that age, they pair, male and female and female with male according to their inclination, and for the rest of their time they live in a pious and law-abiding way. Faithfully adhering to the agreements which were the beginning of their love.

But, is the fact that Plato defends monogamy in the *Laws*, decreeing that the citizens get married, sufficient to exclude homosexual relations between men? What does Plato actually accept? Does he accept homosexual actions only for pleasure, or does he accept them if they make us become more wise and so justify their existence if and only if they contribute to our wisdom? We are inclined to accept the latter alternative; the first one is surely impossible, as we have just shown. By making men get married or forcing them to get married by the imposition of fines, Plato does not necessarily show that men would be happy – which is the main aim of constructing this state – if they felt differently inside them. Forcing them to get married is somewhat wrong, as women could be the victims of any such engagement because of the disloyalty and unfaithfulness of their husbands. However, as we have already stressed above, the wives are viewed as nothing more than productive machines (bring up and raise children – domestic sphere) and men, though married, are by nature as Plato understands it, led towards people like them with whom they can talk etc. If someone feels fascinated by the wisdom of his equal he will fall in love. However, in the *Laws*, more explicitly than in any other Platonic dialogue, Plato condemns the consummation of homosexual desire and love on the ground that they are contrary to nature. This requires men to be with women for the purpose of procreation, and so making society survive and continue to exist. Yet in other dialogues Plato understands that homosexuality is likely to exist.

I believe that what all Platonic dialogues have in common as regards the very existence and justification of homosexuality is that Plato never advocates physical sexual intercourse between men. Thus, the *Laws'* views on homosexuality can be seen as the culmination of Plato's previous views on the

---
[126] Plato, *Laws*, 773.

subject, if the *Laws* is indeed the last of Plato's works. If so, then Plato really is in accord with his previous thought, and the Aristotelian commentary of the *Laws* has proved to be accurate not only in this issue but on the majority of issues discussed in the *Laws*, which we have already stressed and discussed.

Female Homosexuality

In discussing female homosexuality, one needs to distinguish clearly between (a) evidence of women loving women (Sappho, Plutarch), (b) evidence of women being sexually deprived (Medea, Lysistrata), and (c) evidence of and speculation about women having sexual relationships with men other than their husbands (e.g. Plutarch's account of Sparta).

The tradition of Sappho as a woman lover appears during the first period of 'middle' comedy. Until that time, none of the ancients, not even Plato, dealt with this kind of love. In the *Symposium*,[127] Plato tells us

> ...but the woman who is a slice of the original female is attracted by women rather than by men – in fact she is a lesbian – while men who are slices of the male are followers of the male, and show their masculinity throughout their boyhood by the way they make friends with men and the delight they take in lying beside them and being taken in their arms.

Although in this passage of the *Symposium* Plato does not discuss extensively this kind of lesbian love, he refers to it, and that could well imply his reference to Sappho.

At least some comedies ascribed to Sappho were written during the fifth century. However, from these titles we can conclude nothing precise about the poet, though their intention might have been to portray Sappho as a *hetaira*, as a free and intellectual woman. The objectivity of the remarks of the poets can be doubted, as it is generally given in scholarship that in the Greek theatre and comedy in particular, we could not have an objective portrayal of reality. Thus if comedy was our only source regarding Sappho's lesbianism we would justifiably doubt the *para physin eros* in which she is said to have been involved. But we could not argue against her lesbianism if we look at Sappho's poetry, where there appear to be some strong feelings towards other women, in spite of the fact that she never explicitly mentions lesbianism or homosexuality in it. Yet, I appreciate that the tendency to identify her as a lesbian poet must have

---

[127] Plato, *Symposium* 191e.

partly been caused by the fact that, on the whole, women in Lesbos, Sappho's birthplace, especially intellectual women, were surrounded by other young women, just as Socrates was surrounded by young boys in Athens. These intellectual women were mainly concerned with the education of the young, and paid particular attention to music and poetry. As Sappho was working on these subjects she herself calls her house *moisopolon*.[128] She could well have been surrounded by other younger women.

Maximos Tyrios[129] tells us that other women in Lesbos, like Gorgo and Andromeda, were also exercising the same role as Sappho. For this reason, Sappho is said to have been sorrowful about her pupil Atthis who left her for Andromeda. The latter appears to have been Sappho's opponent. In her own ode to Aphrodite,[130] Sappho, tells her:

> ...and what I most wished to happen to myself in my maddened heart. Whom am I to persuade the time to lead her back to your love who wrongs you Sappho? If she turns away, soon she shall pursue- if she does not accept gifts, why she shall give them instead- and if she does not love, soon she shall love even against her will.

Sappho goes on to request the Goddess to come to her '...now and deliver me from oppressive anxieties all the fulfilment my heart longs for fulfil; and you yourself be my fellow fighter'.

In *Desire*[131] Sappho expresses the emotions associated with love's madness and connecting the latter to a real situation. She tells us:

> For when I look at you for a moment; then it is no longer possible for me to speak, my tongue has snapped, at once a subtle fire has stolen beneath my flesh. I see nothing with my eyes, my ears hum, sweat pours from me, a trembling seizes me all over, greener than grass I am, and it seems to me that I am little short of dying.

Although we do not know whether Sappho identifies the poor with a female, we presume she does imply it, if we consider the grammar of the poem carefully.

---

[128] Sappho, *Poems and Fragments*, 136.
[129] Maximos Tyrios XXIV, F41.
[130] Sappho, *Poems and Fragments: The Goddess of Love*, 78–79, 20–21.
[131] Sappho, *Poems and Fragments: Desire*, 20–21.

Plutarch[132] also may give us some evidence of women loving women. 'Women', he tells us, 'of good repute were in love with girls'. But, as modem scholarship is often in doubt about Plutarch's reliability as a historian, we may either not trust it completely, or at least should be cautious about it. As regards our second point about women being sexually deprived, we may take into consideration the examples of Medea and Lysistrata. In the case of Medea we hear her say that her husband had defiled her bed with another woman, while in *Lysistrata*[133] we hear Lysistrata complain about her many sleepless nights, suggesting the sexual starvation of married women in classical Greece.

I am aware that Medea is angry when she makes the above statement, whilst *Lysistrata* is a comedy. But on the whole one may suppose, if not be certain of, the likelihood of all-female relationships, as women were deprived to some extent of sexual intercourse with their husbands. In view of their dissatisfaction, there might have been some lesbian relationships among sexually deprived women. However, this is more of a supposition than an actual fact, at least as far as the women of Athens are concerned. The latter were educated in a different way from those in Sparta and other Dorian states, and had less freedom. Women in archaic Mytilene in Lesbos, and in Sparta, had more opportunities to establish lesbian relationships, partly because of their freedom in comparison with women in Athens.

As to the question of whether Athenian women could possible enjoy homosexual relationships with either their slaves or prostitutes or other women in general, that we cannot know. What we do know and may take for granted is Medea's[134] remark that:

> ...we women are the most unhappy kind. First we must throw our money to the wind, to buy a husband and what's worse, we have to accept him as the old master of our body... To please this stranger who is in your bed... A man who's tired of what he gets at home, goes out and gives his heart a holiday.

Medea does not explicitly tell us here about homosexuality; she could equally be talking about *hetairai* (courtesan) and *pornai* (prostitutes). Nevertheless, we have sufficient reason to think that she implies it when she says that it is legitimate for man to 'give his heart a holiday', as man in classical Greek

---

[132] Plutarch, *On Sparta*, 18,9.
[133] Aristophanes, *Lysistrata*, 26–28.
[134] Euripides, *Medea*, 229–248.

culture often gave himself a holiday. In other words, when he felt he had had enough at home, he could go out and find the company of *his philos*, or generally of another man with whom he could even fall in love, as it was an accepted fact, a contemporary social phenomenon, for equals to fall in love with equals.

As regards the question of whether women could have sexual relationships with men other than their husbands, we are told by Plutarch, in his account of Spartan life, that women in Sparta had absolute freedom, and that on the whole the family in Sparta was organised in a completely different way from that in Athens.[135]

Spartan women were allowed to have sexual relationships with men other than their husbands. What concerned the community was the birth and upbringing of healthy children who would be useful and serve the state. Besides, that was the main expectation of the family. As Plutarch notes, under such a system the existence of *moicheia* (μοιχεία) could not even be conceived. In short, Plato's position in the *Laws* is quite similar to that of Plutarch in that '...at an appropriate age they pair off, the male picks a wife and female chooses a husband and for ever afterwards they live in a pious and abiding way'.[136]

---

[135] Plutarch, *On Sparta*, 15,16.
[136] Plato, *Laws*, 840, 780, 805.

Chapter III
Gods, Heroes and the Theocracy of *Laws* IV

Ancient Greek religion before Plato was characterised by the 'anthropomorphism' of the Gods who had been introduced during the religious quest of the Greeks throughout the ages. The Gods, however, differed from human beings in that they were immortal and unchangeable through all time. Nevertheless, they resembled mankind in the sense that, like mortals, they had passions, emotions and weaknesses. They could fall in love, express hate, feel jealous and be forgiving. Above all, they were thought to be near to men, and to be influenced by those who tried to appease them with sacrifices and prayers.

In addition to the Olympian and Chthonic Gods, the Greeks worshipped a large number of demigods, known as heroes, among whom were Theseus, the most beloved of Athenian heroes, and Heracles, the great Peloponnesian hero. These heroes could in some ways be said to be like saints are for us today, as they were beings with admirable qualities who were regarded as divine after their death.

By the time of Aeschylus, Zeus had become the principal moral power and moral standard of the Greeks and was thought to have helped mankind to reach the perfection of classical times. Euripides, in *The Trojan Women*[1], makes Hecuba address Zeus in the following way:

> O you who support the earth and who have your seat upon earth, whoever you are, difficult to fathom and to understand, Zeus whether inflexible law of nature, or man's mind, I call upon you following your path soundlessly you direct the affairs of men in accordance with justice.

---
[1] Euripides, *The Trojan Women*, 886.

In this way he makes Hecuba express a belief in divine justice. However, by the time of Euripides the Greeks had started to question the existence and nature of the Olympian Gods for two main reasons. First, there had been an introduction of other modes of thought, as a result of the Sophistic movement. Second, foreign religions, and the Orphic and Dionysiac cults in particular, had by now been introduced into Greece and naturally had an impact on both the dramatists and philosophers of the time.

Isis, Serapis, Harpokrates, Anoubis, and other Egyptian Gods seem to have been introduced to Athens in the fourth century BC, mostly by traders coming into Piraeus. 'Resolved by the people to give the merchants of Kition (from Cyprus) the right to own a piece of property in which they are to found a sanctuary of Aphrodite, just as the Egyptians are establishing the sanctuary of Isis.'[2] Once installed, the Egyptian Gods enjoyed great popularity in and around the city of Athens. Even though their shrines lay beyond the limits of the Athenian *agora*, a great number of small objects have been found.

The Orphic cult[3] had a great impact on Plato, as his dialogues allow us to see. Indeed, Plato adopted a number of Orphic beliefs. Alongside this inclination, Plato was influenced by Pythagoreanism, which also had a strongly religious aspect. The most obvious evidence of the significance of Pythagorean mathematics in Athens is the architectural plan of the Parthenon of 448 BC, which required a theory of geometrical proportions. Indeed, Plato's discussion of the immortality and reincarnation of the soul in *Phaedo*, the mathematics basis for the structure of the universe in *Timeaus* and his admiration for monotheistic sun-worship all show Orphic and/or Pythagorean influence.

In spite of the fact that in his dialogues Plato expressed great respect for divine justice, he was nevertheless fully conscious of the difficulties and limits involved in dealing with religious questions. He writes in *Timeaus*,[4] 'But the

---

[2] IG II², 337, decree of 333–2 BC – *Gods and Heroes in the Athenian Agora* (1980), picture book no. 19, prepared by John McK. Camp II. Produced by the Meriden Gravure Company, Meriden, Connecticut, American School of Classical Studies at Athens 1980.

[3] Kern, 1921, p.91. According to Kern, when Plato speaks of the ancient legends in the Laws, he means the Orphic. In the Orphic cosmogony Zeus was eternal, immortal the first and the cause of everything. This idea was in contrast to the School of Miletus (sixth century BC) that taught that the cause and *arche* of everything was water (Thales), the infinite (Anaximander) or the air (Anaximenes). The Orphics viewed soma as the 'envelope of the soul' (Plato, *Cratylus*, 400c).
See also Plato, *Phaedo*, 69c, where Plato is evidently influenced by the Orphic idea that justice is a kind of individual purification, and De *Mundo*, a work of Aristotle whose authenticity is disputed. In this work it is said that Zeus is the *aitia* of everything. In the Laws (716a), this view is commemorated.

[4] Plato, *Timeaus*, 28c.

father and maker of all this universe is past finding out and even if we could find him to tell of him to all men would be impossible'.

Plato knows that in the world where he lives there are men who hold the views expressed by Glaucon and Adeimantus in the *Republic*. [It must be noted here that these figures are not presented as really holding these views, only as putting them up for Socrates to argue against.] Thus, for Glaucon in *Republic* II, justice or morality is a compact of convenience. For Adeimantus, men only value justice for the reward it brings in terms of a good reputation in society and in the world beyond, for the Gods reward the just. He thus considers the Gods as anthropomorphic creatures, whilst stating that it is possible for individuals who commit wrong to avoid punishment by making sacrifices in the community where they live. Above all, Plato knows that human nature may be ignorant and so to tell people about what God really is would be a difficult task, in the same way that it would be difficult for the philosopher who was made to leave the cave and see the objects which before he had seen only as shadows, to tell his former fellow prisoners what he had seen. The philosopher needs to grow accustomed to the light before he can see the new reality of life beyond the cave. Plato then tells us that he will be required to go back into the cave in order to share his knowledge with the unenlightened. But to convince them of it will be impossible, as all they have been able to see until now, have been shadows which they have taken to be realities.[5]

In *Phaedrus*[6] Plato also notes that the ideas men have formed about God are products of their imagination, and are not based on actual reality, but rather on their misunderstanding and misconception of what appears to them to be reality:

> This composite structure of soul and body is called a living being, and is further termed 'mortal'; 'immortal' is a term applied on no basis of reasoned argument at all, but our fancy pictures the God whom we have never seen, not fully conceived, as an immortal living being possessed of a soul and a body united for all time.

Feeling the spiritual power of God, Plato rejected 'anthropomorphic' Gods. However, as he appreciated that a divine being could neither be described with precision nor be symbolised with one symbol only, he made use of the names given to the Gods of the religions prevalent in Greece in his time, most

---

[5] Plato, *Republic*, 516 ff. (The allegory of the cave).
[6] Plato, *Phaedrus*, 246c.

notably in *Cratylus* where he gives (ironic) etymologies of the names of the Gods. Above all, in certain dialogues, like *Timeaus* and the *Laws*, Plato developed the idea that between God and the material world there is a middle substance, the world soul. In the myth of *Politicus*,[7] Plato notes that God sometimes turns away his face from the world. Indeed, both the idea for the world soul and the point from *Politicus* are arguments against pantheism. For this reason, I believe that we cannot regard Plato as a pantheist, as pantheism treats God as identical to the world: God for them is in everything and everywhere.

In *Timeaus*[8] Plato tells us that the world is not born out of *meden* (zero, nothing), but is born out of already existing elements which God puts in a harmonious order '...wherefore also finding the whole visible sphere not at rest but moving in an irregular and disorderly fashion, out of disorder, he brought order, considering that this was in every way better than the other'.

Thus, for Plato, the cause of all harmony in the world is God, the *demiourgos theos* (the creator of all things) as 'when he was forming the universe, he put intelligence in soul, and soul in body, that he might be the creator of a work which was by nature fairest and best', Plato goes on to say that the world is '...a living creature truly endowed with soul and intelligence by the providence of God'. Thus, for Plato, God should not be conceived as an anthropomorphic or physical God, but as a manifestation of spiritual power that influences the physical world, whilst aiming at bringing harmony and preserving it in the world. Plato assumed that every individual should pay respect to the spiritual power that was above him, and was the *arche* of everything in the world in which he lived. The individual who failed to pay his respects to the divine would be no more than a useless member of his political community, as his life would be far from being religious. He would contribute nothing to the collective values, the good and the *eudaimonia* of his community. Indeed, it was the community that mattered to Plato, as it did to any other member of any city state of the fifth and fourth century.

This concern for the preservation of collective values and the collective good are counter to the traditional Greek myths, which were mostly concerned with the heroic and thus placed stress and emphasis on the individual. Plato objects to them for that reason. He also takes issue with the traditional Greek myths in so far as they express the values of the community: Plato

---

[7] Plato, *Politicus*, 268e–274e.
[8] Plato, *Timeaus*, 29d–92c.

thinks the community has the wrong values. He wants to change both these values and the myths.

Tragedy, which used these myths, was partly concerned with the greatness of the mythical heroes and partly with the social, political, religious and moral issues of fifth century Athens, where the idea of collectivism was most apparent. 'Tragedy is a debate with a past that is still alive', as Jean-Pierre Vernant[9] puts it, and it '...confronts heroic values and ancient religious representations with new modes of thought that characterise the advent of law within the city state'. Tragedies conveyed their themes through myths of the past. As these placed considerable importance on individual human power, they could be seen as leading people to atheism. Hence Plato criticised existing Greek mythological modes of thought both in the *Laws* and notably in the *Republic*, in spite of the fact that his own dialogues contained myths. More precisely, in his dialogues Plato very often criticised either directly or indirectly the use made of Greek myths, although he realised that they expressed the collective social consciousness, that is, the way of life and values of the community as a whole. This criticism is most noticeable in *Republic* II, III and X, in which Plato tells us about the kind of education that guardians should receive. Plato, knowing that every schoolboy of his time was reading Homer and learning passages by heart, tells us that most existing poetry ought to be avoided. He believed that contemporary poetry was leading the audience towards a false idea of the Gods. Indeed, tragedy was borrowing heavily from the stories told by Homer. Aeschylus was said to have called his plays 'rich slices from the banquet of Homer'.[10] Thus, the audience would inevitably accept the idea of Gods as anthropomorphic beings, an idea conventionally accepted by the poets. In contrast, Plato conceived of Gods as being *perfectly* good, and as beings that do not change form or mislead us by deceit.

It is worth reminding ourselves that Plato's criticism of traditional Greek myths was not as provocative as it may appear at first glance. He was not the first to attempt to offer a rationalistic criticism of mythology. Xenophanes had attacked anthropomorphic representation of the Gods, and Euhemerus had argued that myths were to be explained as stories about men who had been deified. Heraclitus, attacked Homer and Hesiod for their dependence on myth.

The tragedians, Euripides in particular, despite using Greek myths as the plots for their plays, sometimes questioned the justice and even the existence

---

[9] Vernant, 1971.
[10] Athenaeus, *Deipnosophists*, 347e.

of the Olympian Gods, probably because they were expressing the religious ideas that were prevalent in the Greece of their day. Here the reader might require an explanation about Plato's own consistency and use of myths in his dialogues, in view of his criticism of traditional Greek myths. Plato was well aware of the Greek myths about cosmogonies, the founding of cities, the causes of laws and the ancestry of kings, in which relationships between Gods and men are portrayed, and he sometimes used such myths. However, his own myths were, on the whole, very different from the type of mythological narrative current in Greek thought. Plato's myths are skilful, deliberate, literary creations, indeed products of his very conscious *techne* in philosophy, that is, 'the most beautiful and greatest of the harmonies' and 'would most justly be said to be the greatest wisdom'.[11] In *Gorgias*[12] Plato tells us to 'Indeed hear [as] they assert a very beautiful *logos*, which you will regard [to be] a *mythos*, as I believe, but I, a *logos*', and so states explicitly that there is a clear difference between *mythos and logos* while understanding that it is possible for people to take one for the other. For Plato, *logos* here is what gives a true account whereas *mythos* offers a false one. The fact that there are Platonic myths that are partially true and partially false does not refute the above distinction between *mythos and logos*, as Platonic myths are of a different kind.[13] However, Plato himself defines myth in different ways: as lacking a *logos;* as being the genus of which *logos* is a species; as being exposed to *logos;* as being the same as *logos;* as the *epideixeis* of true beings, or as the account of genesis of a phenomenon as most explicitly designated myths in Plato's works show. As Plato is not entirely consistent in his definition of *mythos* and how the latter differs from *logos*, I will be following a modern classification of the two terms, paying attention to what Plato does with myths, rather than to how he distinguishes them from *logos* and how he defines them. 'In fact genesis is the very soul of any myth', Jacob Klein[14] tells us. He goes on:

> To understand the world, the story of its genesis has to be told. To understand the Gods, the story of their genesis has to be told. Cosmogony and theogony are the primary subjects of any myth. In order properly to understand any event in human life or the character of a people or a city, the event and the character have always to be related, it seems, to their mythical origins. To tell the myth of something means to tell how

---

[11] Plato, *Laws*, III 689d.
[12] Plato, *Gorgias*, 523a1–2.
[13] Plato, *Laws*, 636b–7e4, 666b, 645c3.
[14] Klein, 'Aristotle: an Introduction' in Crossey, 1954, p.58.

this something came to be. An enterprise of this kind does not make much sense unless one relates everything ultimately to beginnings which make any genesis possible.

Thus, whilst conceiving of Platonic myths as speeches about the genesis of a phenomenon, I also intend to stress that they had an intimate relation to Plato's intention and to the purpose of the dialogue in which they were contained. Platonic myths themselves contained many important philosophical ideas. Yet Plato used myths when he wanted to remain vague and unclear, as asserting something of which he was not certain would give rise to philosophical problems and arguments. For a better appreciation and understanding of the place of myths in Plato's dialogues, anyone interested in the subject ought to take as his starting point that there is always an intimate connection between the place and meaning of a myth and the content, context and purpose of a dialogue as a whole.

A careful reading of Plato's dialogues makes clear to the reader that in *Protagoras*, a first period dialogue, *mythos and logos* appear to coincide, although it is true to say that *mythos was* basically performing a 'decorative' function such as it also performed for the Sophists. Nevertheless, the myth put in Protagoras' mouth is about the genesis of the universality of justice, modesty and political virtues in general. In the dialogues constructed during the peak of Plato's philosophical career, myths, though usually to be found at the end of the work, were mostly designated myths about the genesis of a phenomenon. I also appreciate that several of them concern eschatology: life after death. Yet a number of them had something else in common, that is, *eros*, as they were concerned with progress towards enlightenment and thus with finding the proper *paideia*.

Religious motives were in Plato's mind when constructing his myths, and this is the case in the *Laws*, where both myths and paramyths are used in order to secure and preserve the lawful behaviour of the Magnesian. To this end Plato even uses lies similar to the political lies he allows the guardians of the *Republic* to use.[15] Indeed he uses confidence-inspiring lies that are intended to mitigate fears in order to persuade the Magnesians in a general way to transform their diseased opinions into healthy ones. Myths and paramyths – Plato makes use of both nouns interchangeably in the *Laws* – are antidotes against atheism and against private accumulation. At the same time, they allow Plato to stress that *logos* and philosophy, which in the *Republic* are to be found in the

---

[15] Plato, *Republic*, III 414b–8, 415d–8.

philosopher–kings, and now in the members of the Nocturnal Council, should not die; what ought to die is ancient Greek mythology. The fact that Platonic myths and paramyths in particular can involve lies does not necessarily imply that they are incorrect; the reverse is quite possible. Similarly, traditional Greek myths could well be partially true and partially false like the Platonic myths, as myth, at least in the case of Plato, did not necessarily imply the giving of a false account.

In the *Laws*, however, unlike other dialogues, though Plato clearly has a good knowledge of Greek mythology, he hardly makes use of it, except when strictly necessary.[16] He tells us, 'I for my part have promised to join in with this piece of fiction I'm now relating', but he then goes on to say that, 'I also intend to give you actual help along those lines so far as I can', whilst stressing his belief that he would be guided by God. After Book IV, in which Plato gives us the genesis of the optimum regime,[17] of cities;[18] and of poetic irony,[19] it is true to say that, considering the length of the *Laws*, he avoids on the whole using even his own myths and paramyths possibly due to his intention to stress that mythology of all kinds ought to be avoided.

When Plato uses myths, which of their nature are both vague and flexible, he allows the audience to consider various possibilities, even if he himself has a clear idea which he wishes to convey. Thus, an audience, whether in the theatre or reading or listening to a Platonic dialogue, could well take the same myth and interpret it in different ways. The myth, or the allegory, of the cave, for instance, has been interpreted differently by different scholars as either ethical or political, as a journey to education and enlightenment, as a mere hypothesis and even as history.[20] I see no reason why Plato's contemporary audience should not have interpreted the myth in more than one way.

In the *Laws*, Plato, seeking precision and exactness, understands the need to avoid using any kind of myth when the description of Magnesia starts. Indeed, he makes note of myths only when necessary, and even when he does, the myths used all have something else in common as well as the fact that they are all concerned with the genesis of a phenomenon. They are all about the origin of psychological phenomena and aspects of human behaviour. Thus, we may see that they are concerned with the genesis of marriage,[21] of habits,[22] of guilt,[23]

---

[16] Plato, *Laws*, VI 752a–b.
[17] Ibid., 711b–712a7.
[18] Ibid., 712e9–714b2.
[19] Ibid., 719a7–720a2.
[20] Plato, *Republic*, 514; Reeve, 1988, pp.50 ff. See also Cross and A.D. Woozley, 1964.
[21] Plato, *Laws*, VI 773b4 ff.

and of blame.[24] This is because the plan proposed in this dialogue is intended to be one that could readily be adopted in an actual state. It is a plan that does not allow the audience to choose, as the three interlocutors of the discussion have already decided on it, through a reasoning process that was indirectly governed by God.

The God Plato has in mind is one that is not possessed of a soul and a body, but is the spiritual power that guides the physical world. Indeed, Plato aims at this stage of his philosophical career to give birth to a new kind of Greek citizen who would be morally strong and would neither fear death nor lack self-control.[25] He wishes to educate this citizen from the time of his birth until his death, making him appreciate, from the time he was in his mother's womb and in his early childhood, the existence of God or Gods as revealed by the visible world and the necessity to pay respect to the divine. Above all, he aims at showing to the new citizen that the world ruler is *theios nomos* (divine law) and that law, though apparently made by humans is in fact the earthly expression of the divine law. Thus, laws are products of a divine governance, and the government of the new city would literally be 'government by God', though this does not imply that Magnesia would be governed directly by God or Gods. Thus, we may call the form of government of Magnesia a 'theocracy'.[26]

The same concern with divine government appears in earlier books of the *Laws*. So I will be moving back to earlier books before the rejection of myth in Book VI.[27]

In order to begin the discussion about law and government, the Athenian suggests that his companions appeal to God to help them with their concern as to what form of government, would be best suited to the new state. Would they adopt one of the existing forms of government like kingship or that in force in either Crete or Sparta? As the third book reveals, in the latter two states the forms of government were actually mixed ones and, as such, better than all other existing forms of government in Greece in Plato's time. In Book III, when explaining the genetic nature of civilisation, he stresses the

---

[22] Plato, *Laws*, VII 790b8, 809b3–812b.
[23] Ibid., IX 865d3–866z.
[24] Ibid., XII 943D4–944C4.
[25] See also the end of chapter I.
[26] Plato, *Laws*, D713c ff., D713d–e, D715d.
[27] Ibid., VI 752a–d.

eudaimonic advantages of living collectively. This idea is also well expressed in the form of myth elsewhere in the *Laws*.[28] Plato tells us that:

> Cronos was of course aware that, as we have explained, no human being is competent to wield an irresponsible control over mankind without becoming swollen with pride and unrighteousness, Being alive to this he gave our communities as their kings and magistrates, not men but spirits, beings of diviner and superior kind, just as we still do the same with our flocks of sheep and herds of other domesticated animals... he set over us this superior race of spirits who take charge of us with no less ease to themselves than convergence to us providing us with peace and mercy, sound law and unscathed justice and endowing the families of mankind with internal concord and happiness.

I take the central and true meaning of this myth to be that the highest power in the state is that of the *theion* (God, divine). God, being immortal, rules the community and so regulates everything concerning it, while *logos and nous* must arrange its legislation. The latter must not be arranged by any citizen, any oligarchy or any democracy that might tend to favour the desires of either the few or the many. Plato understands that when those who are in power either abolish existing laws or put forward new ones according to their desires and interests, the state will neither be preserved nor survive.

Plato then makes the Athenian remind his companions as well as his audience of the current sophistic view of law.[29] There are different kinds of laws, in the same way as there are different kinds of states: different laws for kingship, democracy, oligarchy and so forth. At this point, there is no disagreement between the interlocutors as to the ultimate purpose of legislation, that is, whether legislation must aim at war and bravery or towards *arete* in general, as all this has been discussed before and agreements had already been reached. However, what we notice here is the conviction of the interlocutors that the form of government and legislation are the means which those who are in power use to preserve this power, and in doing so preserve their own interests. The criterion that *dikaion* in these states is based upon, is the interest of the stronger. This view *peri dikaiou* (about justice) has already been expressed by Plato in *Laws* III: 'And fifth I conceive for the stronger to rule, and for the weaker to submit'. He sees this as prevalent even in the animal king-

---

[28] Plato, *Laws*, IV 713 ff.
[29] Ibid., IV 714b.

dom, as Pindar has also said. However, the Athenian says that they felt that the highest and most important of all the claims was the sixth one, 'which prescribes that it is for the ignorant to follow and for the wise men to take the lead and rule'.[30]

He goes on to say that '...it is just this, this enforced rule of law over willing subjects by all accomplished Pindar, that I cannot pronounce unnatural. I should call it nature's own ordinance'.

Having offered this theoretical discussion and the historical narrative in particular, Plato has explained to his audience the disastrous consequences any state would incur if it allowed itself to be the instrument of those in power. Plato stresses that its citizens would neither be healthy nor its laws fair (just), as the latter would serve only the interest of one class rather than those of the whole community. Those states which have laws based on the interests of the few are 'prone to sanction'; indeed, anomalous and destructive forms of government. Thus, although it is essential to have laws, the rulers of the state should not be more than their servants and slaves.[31]

The Athenian imagines the new colonists under the establishment of their political leaders, and with the consent of his companions he starts his *logos* that constitutes the general preamble of legislation. According to the Orphic *logos*, says the Athenian, God has in his hands the beginning and the end as well as the means of all being. God is always accompanied by *dike and dikaiosyne* which punish all those who offend his law. Only the individual who obeys and respects God's law can hope for the fulfilment of his wishes and of his *eudaimonia;* the individual who offends God's law is punished unquestionably. Man is led towards *paranomia* because of his concern with wealth, honours, the beauty of his body, his youth, or his foolishness. Thus, in order to preserve harmony in the state, he must be punished.

In *Gorgias*[32] also, Plato tells us that the divine law does not accept either disturbance or offence. Not man, but God, is the measure of all things. By asserting the above, Plato denies the idea of Protagoras that viewed man as the measure of all things. For Plato, man must try to be like God,[33] as far as this is possible within the limits of humanity, an idea that was also stressed in *Theaetetus* where Plato talks of the *omoisis theo* (resemblance/similarity to God). This striving of man to be like God must be a reflection of his *sophrosyne*, temperance: 'He that is temperate among us is loved by God, for he is like

---

[30] Plato, *Laws*, III 690b.
[31] Ibid., IV 715d.
[32] Plato, *Gorgias*, 507e.
[33] Plato, *Laws*, 716e.

God, whereas he that is not temperate is unlike God and at variance with him, so also it is with the unjust and the same rule holds in all else'.[34]

In the *Sophist*[35] Plato tells us that, 'The Sophist takes refuge in the darkness of not being, when he is at home and has the lack of feeling his way, and it is the darkness of the place that makes him so hard to perceive'. He goes on to say that, '...whereas the philosopher whose thoughts constantly dwell upon the nature of reality is difficult to see because his region is so bright for the eye of the vulgar soul cannot endure to keep its gaze fixed on the divine'.

In the same work, discussing the *pantelos on*[36] Plato attributes to the latter the characteristic epithet 'divine', whilst wishing once again to justify the view that the 'divine' was worthy and ought to receive our highest respect. This idea was indeed in Plato's mind when constructing *the Laws*. What Plato does at this stage of the *Laws* is to explain the necessity of putting across precise legislation with preambles so that he can create his theocracy. Each preamble[37] will, in turn, perform a kind of theoretical introduction to the law proposed. But the preambles are also needed for another purpose, that is, that legislation is a way of educating the citizens. However, the Platonic way of education is not like that of the poets. Mimetic poetry does not lead towards the truth which is one but about one thing there might be two or three *logoi*. This is in fact contra to Plato's idea about the truth.[38] In order to do that, Plato urges the legislator to prepare the citizens to accept the *Laws* through artful preambles, comparing the good legislator with the freeman's doctor who does not proceed to the administration of a therapy before he has thoroughly discussed the matter with his patient and convinced him.[39] The legislator must describe his laws in an exact and precise way, and without the possibility of them being doubted and interpreted differently by different people. In this way, as we have seen, he ought to discard any mythological narrative in his plan. The latter, for Plato, simply encouraged moral weaknesses such as fear of death and lack of self control, in contrast to Plato's aim to make the new citizens moderate by making them show devotion to the God or Gods and honour them at all times, especially on occasions of public worship.

Plato was of course aware that the Athenian year was full of days set aside for religious activities. He knows that the Hellenic festivals were basically

---

[34] Plato, *Theaetetus*, 176 b–d.
[35] Plato, *Sophist*, 254a.
[36] Ibid., 249a–e.
[37] Plato, *Laws*, 718b.
[38] Ibid., 725d.
[39] Ibid., IV 719 ff.

religious festivals which, apart from providing good entertainment with lavish processions, theatrical and choral performances and athletic contests, placed a substantial emphasis on worshipping the Gods. Many of the festivals took place in a holiday atmosphere, and the whole population would partake of the religious life of the city. As there was no separation between state and church in ancient Greece, Plato understood that the new city of Magnesia would itself be the focus of religious life. Hence, all religious activities would be carried out under the protection of her laws. The laws made by the three interlocutors therefore had to describe precisely the arrangements and conduct of the festivals in the state, and which sacrifice should be made for which Gods, but always with the help of the Oracle. Hence, Plato lists everything that belongs to the jurisdiction of the Oracle, the foundation of temples, the enactment of sacrifices, the adoration of Gods, the place of demons and heroes, whilst advising the legislator to ask for the help of the ancestral exegete Apollo. Whether Plato is here describing Delphic customs, as some have suggested, it is hard to say. However, even if he does describe Delphic customs, he certainly does not share all the attitudes that come from Delphi. If we look at *Laws* IX where Plato considers the question of who will be responsible when a wife murders her husband, he emphatically disagrees with the traditional Delphic view. He disagrees with the answer that the son of both the murdered father and the killer mother should kill his mother in return, an attitude that traditionally Apollo would have taken. The God Apollo might have been content with this solution, but Plato, like most people in the fifth and fourth century, Euripides among them, did not accept the logic of this. This was partly because of the establishment of the Areopagus that had abolished the former right and task of the relatives of the man who had been killed to take back his blood whether it had been spilt by accident or in murder. The fact that Plato's view differs from that of Orestes, while being a reflection of the traditional 'Delphic' view, suggests that even if Plato is describing Delphic customs he does not accept them wholeheartedly. Yet, I appreciate that Plato could be said to be in accordance with Apollo's teaching of the *meden agan* (nothing in excess) that is, of not elevating one's own self, but of knowing that every individual is subordinated to the power of the Gods, though of course Plato conceives of God in a different way from Apollo's teaching. What Plato aims at stressing is that the laws of every society are supported by divine authority and the Athenian and his interlocutors now need this authority in their attempt to enact new laws and to determine the relations between men and the Gods. Once the religious laws have been enacted, Plato thinks that they ought to treat erroneous beliefs about God and the unseen world as crimes, in order to abolish atheism. Plato thinks highly of the divine element in the world. His respect for it is explicitly stated, as we have already noted in his description of God as the measure of all things. Thus, it is God who is the *aitia* of the Magnesian *nomoi*, whereas the three interlocutors, even at their best, are perfectly rational beings that are no more than 'copies' or 'puppets' in the hands of the Gods.[40] In this way, Magnesia can only be an imitation of the most beautiful and best life. The justice of Magnesia can only be an image of the pure justice of God that is the *arche* of all things in heaven and on earth and their *telos*.[41]

It is interesting to compare Plato's notion of God with that of Christianity, although the latter is not a metaphysical system. It differs from Platonic thought in its essential relation to and dependence on particular historical events and experiences. Christianity begins with particular non-recurrent historical events that are regarded as revelatory and on the basis of which the Christian faith makes certain limited statements about the ultimate nature and structure of reality. We do not know what Plato would have said if he had known the history of Israel as understood and participated in the prophets and apostles, these events being seen by faith as revelatory of God. Plato, of course, does not argue for the biblical revelation and does not regard any objects such as the cross and the consecrated bread and wine with reverence. However, religion does occupy an important place in the *Laws;* indeed, I take it to be its core and heart.

As we have seen, the concept of religion that Plato aims at showing us is a new one. For this reason, when he starts the dialogue he portrays the era of Zeus, the era in which the interlocutors lived and which had replaced the age of Kronos. Traditionally, in Greek thought, the latter was regarded as a 'golden age', an idea that Plato was making use of in the *Laws*. But as soon as the interlocutors start their legislation for Magnesia, it becomes evident that although God will guide them, they need to place all their emphasis on their power to reason, as reason is the only route to God, the only way to have direct knowledge of the divine reality. And by doing so, they would inevitably understand the necessity for 'the death of Greek mythology'. *Logos* is the only way to help them see that Rhadamantus' *techne* is of no necessity, because God is not what Homer and Hesiod had previously described. The God of the new age that Plato is announcing in the *Laws* is the divine *nous*, *the arche*, the measure of all things, even of human affairs, and is neither that of the era of

---

[40] Plato, *Laws*, 644d.
[41] Ibid., 817d.

Kronos nor that of Zeus. This idea becomes particularly evident at the end of the dialogue when the interlocutors are said never to have reached the cave of Zeus. They have instead been persuaded by their harmonious reasoning process, indirectly guided by the divine *nous*. The laws they have proposed are the earthly expression of *divine nous*, and as such they are the best available. In this way they neither need Zeus nor reach his cave, as, unlike those of the cave as described in the *Republic*, both Kleinias and Megillus are persuaded by the means of reason the Athenian philosopher uses. He, unlike his companions, is aware of the divine *nous*, and that the light is not to be found in the darkness of the cave of Zeus, but, as he has already shown his companions, it can be found in their real life by the correct use of their *logos*. Thus, what Plato actually means by the phrase in the *Laws* that God is the 'measure of all things much more truly than, as they say, man'[42] is that God is *logos* and that *logos* in the material world is to be found in the philosopher, in the *basilikos aner* (βασιλικός ανηρ), who lives according to *logos* in both his individual and his political life, and as such is the means by which *logos* is to be directed and understood by the enlightened. This idea is in total agreement with that of the *Republic*, as those who were made to leave the cave and see the real light had to go back and communicate their knowledge of it to the unenlightened.

The Philosophical Theology of *Laws* X

Kant began the Preface to the first edition of his *Critique of Pure Reason* as follows:

> Human reason has this peculiar fate that in one species of its knowledge it is burdened by questions which as prescribed by the very nature of reason itself it is not able to ignore, but which as transcending all its powers, it is also not able to answer.[43]

And Socrates says in *Theaetetus:*

> If I make no mistake I have heard some people say this: there is no definition of the *primary elements* – so to speak – out of which we and everything else are composed; for everything that exists in its own right can only be *named*, no other determination is possible; neither that it *is* nor that it *is not*... But what exists in its own right has to be ...named

---

[42] Plato, *Laws*, 716c–15.
[43] Kant, translated by Normal Smith, 1929, p.7.

without any other determination. In consequence it is impossible to give an account of any primary element; for it, nothing is possible but the bare name- its name is all it has. But just as what consists of these primary elements is itself complex, so the names of the elements become descriptive language by being compounded together. For the essence of speech is the composition of names.[44]

What both Kant and Plato have in common is that they are both aware of the difficulties that questions in philosophy raise. Wittgenstein writes that, 'You can't say etsch, etsch! to philosophical problems, they are too strong'.[45] The Eleatic stranger (whom I take to represent Plato's view) tells us in the *Sophist*, 'It strikes me that Parmenides and everyone else who has set out to determine how many and what kinds of things exist have spoken to us in quite a careless way. For each of them seems to me to have told us some kind of story as if we were children.[46]

Aristotle commented as follows: The question which has always been asked, is asked now, and always will be asked: 'what is being?' is just the question: 'what is substance?'[47] and he thought of what he sometimes called 'first philosophy' *prote philosophia* as an inquiry about substance; for it is the origins and the causes of substances that are being investigated'.[48] When Aristotle tells us that this is just the question 'what is substance?', he goes on to say, 'For this some claim to be one, others more than one; some claim it is limited in number, others unlimited. And so our chief and first and almost only concern must be to consider what this being (i.e. substance) is'.[49]

However, Aristotle never succeeds in explaining to us how what he says about being in his doctrine of the categories relates to what he says about substance when he distinguishes between three substances. And when he does speak of substance, it means quite different things for him in different places. What does seem to be clear, however, is that Aristotle thinks that what he calls forms are unchanging and eternal, but this does not mean that there are no differences between Platonic and Aristotelian forms. For Aristotle, these are what he calls the simple objects of thought that are referred to in the premises of syllogisms; forms which for Aristotle are definitions of the essence do not

---

[44] Plato, *Theaetetus*, 201e–202c.
[45] Quoted by Rush Rhees, *Human World*, No 3, May 1971.
[46] Plato, *Sophist*, 272c.
[47] Aristotle, *Metaphysics*, 1028b2.
[48] Ibid., 1069a18.
[49] Ibid., 1028b4 ff.

come into existence but are eternal. So it seems that Aristotle does speak of the elements of which we and everything else is made as Plato put it in *Theaetetus*.

F.M. Cornford says of the passage in the *Theaetetus*, 'The theory put forward was certainly never held by Plato', and it may not be difficult to show why this is so.[50] Aristotle tells us of Plato:

> After the systems we have named came the philosophy of Plato, which in most respects followed these thinkers, but had peculiarities that distinguished it from the philosophy of the Italians. For, having in his youth become familiar with Cratylus and with the Heracleitean doctrines that all sensible things are ever in a state of flux and that there is no knowledge of them, he held these views even in later years.

We find confirmation of what Aristotle said in Plato's *Timeaus* where Timeaus says:

> We must then, in my judgement, first make this distinction: what is that which always is and has no becoming, and what is that which is always becoming and never is? That which can be grasped by thought and expressed in words is what is ever the same; whereas that which is the object of belief together with perception that cannot be expressed, is what comes to be and perishes, and never really is.[51]

Plato thought that the pattern that God used to make the world was an unchanging one. He asks: 'After which of the two models did its builder frame it? After that which is always in the same unchanging state, or after that which has come to be?'[52] His answer is:

> Now if this world is good and its maker is good, clearly he looked to the eternal; but if what cannot be said without blasphemy is true, then to the created pattern. Everyone then, must see that he looked to the eternal; for the world is the best of things that have come to be, and he is the best of causes. Having come to be, then in this way the world has been fashioned on the model of that which can be grasped by thought that is expressed in words and is always in the same state.[53]

---

[50] Cornford, 1935, p.143.
[51] Plato, *Timeaus*, 270 ff.
[52] Ibid., 28c–29a.
[53] Ibid., 29a.

But it is not as if Plato thinks that it is possible to give an account of the universe that is exact and accurate, 'For an account is of the same order as the things it sets forth'.[54] So Timeaus tells Socrates:

> If, then, Socrates, in many respects concerning many things – the Gods and the generation of the universe – we prove unable to render an account of all points entirely consistent with itself and exact, you must not be surprised. If we can furnish accounts no less likely than any other, we must be content, remembering that I who speak and you my judge are only human, and consequently it is fitting that we should in these matters accept the likely story and look for nothing further.[55]

However, in the *Laws*, Plato does not present his discussion as a 'likely story' as he wants to be precise about Gods. Indeed, throughout his philosophical career, unlike Aristotle who thought it was possible to give an account of the cosmos and of God which is definite and exact, Plato felt that this was not possible. Nevertheless, he does speak about the sum total of things or the universe as a whole, but thought that its nature could not be made plain. Thus he feels somewhat insecure about giving precise answers to metaphysical questions, as he knows that they are dealing with what is not understood (and what I would say remains not understood). This insecurity and uncertainty of Plato, I believe, may explain at least in part the inconsistencies in *Laws* x where Plato seems as unsure as ever before in his discussion of the world souls, and the soul–body relationship in particular. It is true that he never actually clearly formulates his ideas, but this is a reflection of his view that questions in metaphysics cannot be answered in a simple way. Genuine metaphysics for Plato begins at the development of reason and ends as the justification of reason. It is the philosophers' task to deal with such questions, as without them philosophy would be emaciated. Accordingly, I believe that the interpreter of the Platonic dialogues in general, and *Laws x* in particular, should not concentrate on the number of inconsistencies contained in the discussion, but rather try to grasp what was beyond Plato's understanding, and what his real aim was when constructing this part of the discussion.[56] Book X of the *Laws* is indeed the part of the work where Plato creates 'a philosophical theology' in order to show the Magnesians the importance of the divine authority and their

---

[54] Plato, *Timeaus*, 29b.
[55] Ibid., 29c–d.
[56] See also Introduction.

duty to respect the latter. Above all, an interpreter ought to see whether Plato, in spite of his inconsistencies, manages to put his point across clearly at the end, whilst considering whether there has been any philosopher or writer who has not made digressions and had inconsistencies in his works.

At this point I must express my agreement with Taylor's description of a the *Laws* as 'the foundation of all subsequent natural theology'.[57] Natural theology or religion or theodicy is, in short, a province of philosophy aiming to demonstrate the idea that deity is a mental power, completing that conception by the consideration of moral convictions and sentiments and apart from revelation. However, under no circumstances could Plato be seen as a deist, a term used particularly in the eighteenth century for those who consciously replaced the biblical concept of God with a philosophical one. Rationalist philosophers like Descartes, Spinoza and Leibniz and empiricists like Locke, Berkeley and Hume attempted to reach God respectively by means of reason or by means of experience. They considered either the former or the latter as the only means by which they could gain an understanding of the nature of what exists. Plato, like these philosophers, may have also created a 'philosophical theology', but his quarrel was with traditional Greek religion, unlike the deists' quarrel with Christianity. At any rate, unlike the deists who had 'religion in their pockets', Plato throughout his career and in the *Laws* in particular shows his belief in the divine *nous*, attempting to make his audience give up the follies of Sophistry and the relativism of their views concerning God. In the *Laws* being morally convinced of the immortality of the soul led him to establish the primacy of the soul as the source of all activity. Plato also demonstrated the existence of God/Gods and described the latter as divine, *nous*, *logos*, indeed as what forms the crown of human knowledge.

Properly speaking, the greatest part of *Laws* X[58] is a preamble to the Platonic penal legislation concerning offences against the Gods, mostly of impiety although the discussion of the latter comes towards the end of the book.[59] The offences against the Gods, that is, 'For all verbal or practical outrage offered to the Gods by speech or act',[60] must be attributed to poets, playwrights, rhetoricians, philosophers and soothsayers, whom he sees as collectively responsible for sowing the seeds of atheism and impiety due to their expression of a misleading and false theology, that is, their false ideas about the nature and existence of Gods. People adopting these ideas, possibly

---

[57] Taylor, 1934, Introduction ii.
[58] Plato, *Laws*, X 885b–907d.
[59] Ibid., 907d–910e.
[60] Ibid., 885b.

due to both their ignorance and desire for pleasure, will then become impious.[61] Thus, it will be necessary to investigate the foundations of these ideas in order to allow the truth of the Gods to be revealed.

Being a philosopher, the Athenian is naturally interested in finding the truth about the nature, existence and role of the Gods, knowing that metaphysical questions need to be treated with caution and a rational reasoning process if they are to be answered at all. He takes a different approach from his companions; Kleinias in particular rushes into offering a short and easy answer of proof of the existence of Gods, pointing at the earth, stars, sun, moon and the beautiful order of seasons. For the Athenian, this way of thinking adopted by Kleinias does not actually establish the existence of Gods, but it does underestimate the impious who consider all the above elements of the cosmos as Gods and divine.

It is indeed one of the negative propositions of the impious that the Athenian aims at attacking, as such beings would be incapable of caring in any way for human affairs. The negative propositions of impious theology widely held in Plato's own time were the following:[62] (a) Gods do not exist, (b) they exist but are unconcerned about the world and humanity, and (c) they exist and are concerned, but can be influenced by prayer. The wrongness of the first impious proposition, or of atheism in general, is to be found in the fact that it is grounded on a materialistic theory of the world. For Plato it inevitably leads to scepticism and atheism. Thus, in order to define the superiority of the soul, banish scepticism and pursue truth and accord with his notion of divine *nous as logos*, Plato begins his discussion by telling us that although the holders of this view argue that all things come into being by nature, by change or by art, they nevertheless go on to say that the greatest and most beautiful things – fire, water and earth – are not works of art, but have all come into being by nature and chance. In this way, they regard only the lesser things as works of art, viewing the latter as mortal, in contrast to nature and chance which are immortal. Thus, the atheists hold the view that it is through the motions and mixture of fire, water and earth that the sun, moon and stars have come into being, while the soul comes into being after these things. This view contrasts with that of Plato, who argues that the soul is prior to all heavenly bodies and is, in fact, more than anything else, what governs all changes in bodies. Evidently, the view that the soul is older than the body and is deathless is a

---

[61] Plato, *Laws*, 886a–8b2, 908b4–c1.
[62] Ibid., 885b.

view that was first introduced by Plato in earlier works, but even now at an old age he is still content to hold it and attempts to justify it, by arguments.

Plato feels that the mistaken view of the impious is due to their misunderstanding of the distinction between body and soul. He thus needs to concern himself with the body–soul relationship and will need to show that *soma* is not the first thing that comes into being. It is not the first cause *(proton aition)* of the genesis and decay of the things in the cosmos. Physical motion for Plato is always produced by some antecedent motion, and what has started this process is not body but soul. He goes on to establish the view that there are ten kinds of motion, two of which are fundamental. One of these two fundamental kinds of motion can only move other things and is affected only by the motions of other things, whereas the other can move both itself and other things. Undeniably, the latter kind of motion is prior to all other kinds as it is self-moving, which implies that it has come into being first. When we see that something bodily possess the self moving motion, we say that the thing is alive, says Plato. Similarly, when we observe soul in things we also say that they are alive. As such, Plato identifies the soul with the motion that moves itself which is what has first come into being and with the motion of all things that are.[63] It is '...the movement which is able to move itself' or '...the activity which can activate itself'.[64] This is expanded into '...the first coming-into-being and movement of those things which are, have been and will be together with the sum total of their contraries', on the grounds that '...in every instance it is soul which is responsible for any change and motion they undergo'.[65] 'Soul comes into being prior to body, while body is secondary and derivative with soul governing in the real order of things, and body being subject to governance'.[66] In order to justify his view, Plato takes the sun as his example, stating three possible ways in which the soul might control the body: from within, as does 'our own soul',[67] from without,[68] or by guiding it in some other mysterious way, 'stripped of body and in possession of other wonderful powers'.[69] He states that the soul is indeed indiscernible to the senses, an idea also expressed in earlier dialogues.[70] He continues his argument, because the

---

[63] Plato, *Laws*, 897a–b.
[64] Ibid., 896a1–2.
[65] Ibid., 896a6–8, 896a8–13.
[66] Ibid., 896c1–3.
[67] Ibid., 898f8–10.
[68] Ibid., 898e10–899a2.
[69] Ibid., 899a–24.
[70] Plato, *Phaedo*, 79b12.

mere priority of the soul does not in itself establish the existence of God or Gods. He moves further by asking his companions what kind of soul rules heaven and earth and the whole circuit as he has already declared that the soul is multiple and that there are to be 'at least two souls' in number,[71] one that is fully virtuous and a second one that possesses neither good sense nor virtue. He answers that if the whole motion of heaven and what it contains has a nature like that of the motion, revolution and calculations of the intellect, one must say that the best soul is in charge of the cosmos. However, if the whole motion proceeds in a mad and disorderly way, one must say that the bad soul is in charge. What is important for Plato at this point of his discussion is to be able to demonstrate that the heavens are governed by the good soul and not by the bad one which is described as 'that which is capable of the contrary effect', that is, of evil. However, in his attempt to prove that the world is governed by the good soul, Plato has been viewed as making interpretation of this part of the discussion rather difficult due to the dubious phrases and the imprecise and misleading language he uses.

Plato emphatically divides the world into two particular souls, *ten aristen psychen* (the best soul) and *ten kaken* (the bad soul). However, this distinction of two world souls into the best and the bad may allow the critic aiming at proving the loose writing of the *Laws* to hold that a number of questions remain unanswered by Plato. This is because Plato tells us that there are 'at least two souls' in number, and that it is the good one that governs the world. The hostile critic may object that Plato, later in his discussion, tells us that, 'It would be blasphemy to ascribe the work to anything but a soul or souls – one or more than one – of absolute goodness'.[72] In other words, whether there is one or more than one good soul that governs the world is an unimportant matter for Plato; after all, there is more than one God. What is of importance to him is to demonstrate the importance of the divine authority, and he clearly does succeed in so doing. As for the use of number two, I take it to be nothing more than an indication of multiplicity; he could well have chosen number three and so forth. Plato thinks that the second erroneous belief is based on the view that the Gods are interested neither in small things nor in human affairs. By contrast, Plato himself views God as the greatest creator and artist of the world, who does nothing out of order and is interested in both small and big things. It is fair to say here that Plato does not actually argue for this view;

---

[71] Plato, *Laws*, 896e5–6.
[72] Ibid., 898c7–8

he simply expounds that the world is a work of art in the full meaning of the word:

> He who provides for the world has disposed all things with a view to the preservation and perfection of the whole, wherefore each several thing also, so far as may be, does and has done to it what is meet. And for each and all there are in every case governors appointed of all doing and being affected, down to the least detail, who have achieved perfection even in the minute particulars.[73]

According to what has been quoted above it is rather easy for Plato now to challenge the third erroneous idea about the Gods. The impious think that the Gods 'can be perverted by the receipt of gifts from the wicked'.[74] The Gods, for Plato, are the highest rulers of the world, and justice is indeed their most profound quality without which men would not be able to conceive the harmonious order of both small and big things in the world, including human affairs. Justice for Plato implies the giving of the right penalties, and 'the right penalty is that he who strays from harmony should be brought back to it'.[75] But if the heavens manifest the presence of a 'best type of soul', where is Plato, the bad type of soul to be found in the world? Will it be found in the heavens alongside the good soul? What Plato must be intending to put across by telling us about the world evil soul is nothing more than his affirmation that evil does exist in the world, and that it is to be found in the diseased souls of ignorant men. Plato appreciates that such men will always exist. 'There will always arise people, sometimes more, sometimes less who have this illness', that is, the illness of impiety,[76] that will always arise naturally in any state and so in Magnesia also. When discussing impiety, Plato makes Kleinias describe the law against it as '...the most beautiful and best prelude for all the laws'.[77] Indeed, this statement reinforces my suggestion that the actual nature of the discussion of *Laws* X as a whole is to arrive at the legislation of the law against the atheists, which Plato indeed formulates clearly, since unlike the metaphysical questions it is about something that can be known and it is in fact known. His description of the law of impiety, as stated above, is due to the fact that it is a

---

[73] Plato, *Laws*, 903b–c. The justice of the Gods and the fate of the soul. Aristotle, *On the Heavens*, 271a33. 'God and nature, however, do nothing in vain.'
[74] Ibid., 905d–e.
[75] Plato, *Critias*, 106b.
[76] Plato, *Laws*, 888b.
[77] Ibid., 887b–c.

law concerned with the cure and purification of the souls of the Magnesians who, though they may be naturally good, could often be drawn towards impiety in some way, due to their *amatheia* (ignorance), that is, in fact, the cause of all wrongdoing, '...for the cause of change lies within themselves'.[78] Indeed, this idea can also be found in a passage in the *Republic* where Plato describes the illness of impiety as a diseased state of the soul and makes Socrates call it 'ignorance in the soul'. Thus, spiritual ignorance, not the ignorance of impious words, is 'truly falsehood'; the latter is only its 'after rising image' and '...responsibility lies with the chooser – not with God'.[79]

However, as noted above, Plato appreciates that even if the *Laws* are studied by all the Magnesians, initially as part of their education,[80] there will always arise some impious people in the city. He offers them the opportunity to study the proofs of the *Laws*, along with all the words of the dialogue again in a setting better suited to focusing their attention than a classroom.

The idea that Plato adopts here is certainly different from the usual punishment in Athens, which seems to have been death or exile if we consider the cases of Socrates or Anaxagoras respectively, In contrast, Plato gives the opportunity to both heretics and atheists to receive visits by officials for the next five years with the intention to '...admonish them and ensure their spiritual salvation'. However, after the lapse of the five years, if a man of this kind is thought to have come to his senses he will be released, but if he relapses he will be punished with death. This idea is totally in accord with earlier dialogues, *Gorgias* in particular, where Plato deals with the same issue. This idea that must be derived from Plato's understanding that either during studying the *Laws* which oppose impiety and impious behaviour or through advice the impious will receive from officials, they will manage to tame their *thymos* whilst understanding for themselves the existence of the divine authority and the primacy of the soul as the source of all activity. On the whole, the line of thought that Plato is adopting in the *Laws* about the committal to prison and the facilitation of re-education is a reflection of his general theory of punishment, aimed at rehabilitating criminals whilst attributing different degrees of punishment to different offenders.

Laws X is thus Plato's attempt to offer a philosophical but religious concept of God, indeed a philosophic theology that I see as an artful preamble to his law of impiety. Plato was well aware that the good legislator is like the free-

---

[78] Plato, *Laws*, 863.
[79] Plato, *Republic*, 617e 4–5.
[80] Plato, *Laws*, 809e, 811c–e.

man's doctor who does not proceed to the administration of therapy before he has thoroughly discussed the matter with and convinced his patient. Thus, he urges the Athenian legislator to prepare the Magnesians to accept this law through this skilful preamble concerned with the existence and goodness of the divine authority.

The Good Man in the *Laws:* His Attitude to Pleasure and Honour

A starting point to examine Plato's ethico-psychological notion of the good man in the *Laws* would be to focus attention and begin thinking about the following questions: 'what is the good life or what is the good for Plato, as a rule for the life of the Magnesians? What are the qualities a Magnesian citizen must have in order to lead his life in a proper way and thus contribute to the *eudaimonia* of his state as a whole? What should the attitude of the good man be, namely in relation to *hedone*, (pleasure) and *timé* (honour)?

In different dialogues, Plato seems to offer different accounts of the good, equating it with pleasure in *Protagoras*, with self-control in *Gorgias;* with what he calls the perfection and the harmony of the soul in *Phaedo* and the *Republic* respectively, and with a combination of thought, intellectual activity and pure pleasures which are seen as ingredients of the best life in *Philebus*.

The apparent shifts that the reader of Plato's works may find in his treatment of pleasure depend on what Plato means by 'pleasure' in each context. Moreover, I think that the key to Plato's notion of pleasure is the idea that virtuous behaviour is what is truly pleasant, in contrast to what most people (and philosophers when attacking it) think of as pleasure. This idea is most explicitly stated in the *Republic*.

For Plato in the *Republic*[81] cannot be defined as what is pleasant, for it is the only object of moral knowledge. In order to express his view, Plato develops a tripartite doctrine both within the state and within the soul which shows how desire for pleasure should be controlled. Plato tells us that the spirited nature *thymos* ought to, and in the just person will, take the side of reason against desire. Only the virtuous man's desires are well trained. This man guards himself especially against pleasure or pleasant things, and notices the mistakes he is liable to make if he is unable to control his desire for pleasure. The virtuous man, therefore, is one whose soul makes certain that the orders of reason are carried out and that his desires for bodily pleasures obey. Thus, he reasons to the extent that he has control of his desires. However, a man cannot be just without also being wise, brave and self-controlled. Hence

---

[81] Plato, *Republic*, 509a.

'understanding of oneself' is brought into the discussion again, since understanding of his own workings helps him to control his desires and fight back his tears.

Plato's position is that each person should do his own thing ('τά ἑαυτοῦ πράττειν'). Virtue for Plato is the freedom of the soul, which means that one should do what one really rationally wills; the most free among men is he who does what he wills. Only the virtuous man is happy since only he has his soul in such a condition as to be happy, and knows what pleasure is, so that he brings himself into harmony with pleasures that are pure and correct measure. However, it is in Book IX of the *Republic* that Plato, having already established that the soul of man is composed of three parts, each of which has its own pleasure, attempts to find where the greatest pleasure is located. The philosopher ruled by reason seeks knowledge, the spirited man seeks honour, and the man of appetite seeks fulfilment of appetite, often through riches. Plato concludes that only the philosopher who has tasted the pleasures of all kinds can be a true judge of pleasure: the pleasures of wisdom come first, those of honour second and those of appetite such as riches, third. Also, the philosopher, being in contact with the world of ideas, is the one who can know the essence of true pleasure. By true pleasure Plato means that which is experienced when the soul is harmoniously ordered under the rule of reason. This implies that the more reasonable the desires, the greater the pleasures they will bring. In this way, what is furthest removed from reason is also furthest from law and order, so that the tyrant is not only the most unfree of all men but is further than anyone else from true pleasure. Thus, the philosophers life will undoubtedly be happier than that of the tyrant. And this is why Plato gives philosophers unlimited powers, as he thinks that due to their knowledge of the good they feel it is their duty to make their fellow citizens understand that it is justice and not injustice that pays better.

In *Philebus*,[82] a dialogue probably written at about the same time as the *Laws*, Plato is also concerned with the nature and worth of pleasure, and considers the question whether the 'good' for man cam be identified simply either with pleasurable feeling or with 'thought' or intellectual activity. The result of the discussion between 20e–22d is that neither pleasure nor thought is the good for man. 'The good', whatever it might be, must be something complete and self-sufficient but Plato does not use the form of the good as expressed in the *Republic* (at least as far as 20e–22d goes). What is worth stressing is that Plato's discussion of pleasure now seems to be more realistic,

---

[82] Plato, *Philebus*, 20e–22d.

as he does not offer another parallel between the ideal state and the individual soul but mainly criticises current Greek ideas concerned with the nature and purpose of pleasure. Yet he does not rush into identifying the good with either pleasure or intellectual activity, since neither term would be sufficient for the acquisition of the good for man. Nevertheless, he does conclude that the good or the best life will be one in which both pleasure and thought are found.

In including pleasure, however, we must note that the pleasures Plato has in mind are a selection of 'true' pleasures like the ones described in the *Republic*. These are rationally controlled pleasures, carefully regulated by an intelligence which seeks measures and limits: ingredients in the good life, rather than the pleasures the hedonist Philebus and his friends have in mind. These are processes of relief, and therefore are inevitably mixed with pain. The contrast, for example, between the pleasure of drinking and the 'pleasure' of not being thirsty is important. Plato here insists that the latter is not the best we can hope to achieve, but there are other, pure pleasures. This point is already anticipated *in Republic* IX.

In conclusion, we may say that pleasure in *Philebus* is neither identical with the good for man nor is it the most important element in the good, and yet it is an ingredient in the 'best life'. Pleasure is now not excluded from Plato's account of the good, as he now realises that man cannot go without some pleasure, but he has to be satisfied with the pleasures which he receives as a consequence of his intelligence. In short, the highest life for man is still one of intellectual activity, but tempered by pleasures necessary due to his biological needs.[83] Pleasures, of course, remain at a lower level than thought and knowledge in what constitutes the good life, and Plato adopts neither a hedonistic nor an anti-hedonistic position as 'some' pleasures are good but most are bad. Even if all pleasures were good, none could be the supreme good.

In *Laws* V,[84] Plato is most evidently concerned once again with the use of pleasure and pain as guides to men's actions, attempting to offer an account of the notion of moral and legal responsibility also discussed in some of his other works. Most precisely, in *Laws* IX Plato faces up to the paradox that 'no man does wrong willingly', basing his argument on the assumption that a man only does wrong when in his soul there is not a 'measured balance'. Plato now adds a very careful analysis of the causes of this: a man can do wrong when he is carried away by anger and fear or again when he is overcome by desire and the

---

[83] Plato, *Philebus*, 63–66c.
[84] Plato, *Laws*, V 732d–734.

search for pleasure, or finally, by ignorance.[85] It could be that for Plato all the above are in some way different forms of ignorance. They are forms of ignorance of the evil soul. Ignorance leads to the love of self and inevitably to human blindness, making people believe that their ignorance is their wisdom.

This is in contrast to Plato's notion of the just man in the *Laws*, whom he sees as being rewarded in a future life, whilst for the wicked he says that there are sanctions reserved.[86] As in the *Republic*, the truly good man must have both his soul and body in such a state that there is a 'measured balance'.[87] Man must manifest such balance in himself, and in doing so he is actually imitating God who is the measure of all things, even of human affairs.[88] As man cannot be God, he can at least imitate God as far as his humanity allows him to do so, and it certainly allows him to combine harmoniously two contrary qualities, the *thymoeides* and the *praon* with the use of his reason. If he does not succeed in combining these qualities and so there is an imbalance of parts of his soul this will imply that his soul is 'in the grip of disease'.[89]

The *agathos* for Plato is somebody who behaves according to the way he ought to. *Agathos* is he who avoids loving himself. The love of man for himself is the greatest of all evils.[90] It is a sin that leads man to believe that he knows everything, whereas in reality he knows nothing. This is the worst way to offer *timé* towards his soul that for Plato in the *Laws* is the second most important good, straight after the Gods. Indeed, for Plato, every man must respect and honour his soul as well as the Gods.

The order of Plato's hierarchy of goods is not actually surprising as for the Greeks the *theous sebein* (honouring the Gods) was always placed before that of the *goneas timan* (respecting the parents) that followed it. According to Anaximenes[91] the *goneas timan* is an unwritten *ethos*. Also, Euripides[92] tells us that paying respect to the Gods was always placed before the honouring of parents that followed it. The most extensive order of goods could be said to be that stated by Plutarch.[93] Nevertheless, what is evidently new in Plato's

---

[85] Plato, *Laws*, III 689a.
[86] Ibid., 727d–881a, 870d–e, 904d–e, 927a–b, 959b.
[87] Ibid., 716d, 728d–e.
[88] Ibid., 716c4–5.
[89] Ibid., 714a5–6.
[90] Ibid., e731e.
[91] Anaximenes, Ρητ 1.
[92] Euripides, *Fragments*, 219.
[93] Plutarch, *Moralia* vol. 1, *De liberis educandis* [The Education of Children], 10,7; Aeschylus, *Eumenides,* 545; Euripides, *Fragments* 853.

hierarchy of goods in the *Laws*, is that he stressed the importance of *timé*. He tells us in the *Laws*[94] that this is *theion agathon* (divine good), whereas none of the bad goods is *timion* and so none is worthy of being honoured. To be precise, Plato stresses in Book III, that in order for a city to live and lead its citizens to *eudaimonia* (happiness) there must be rulers who know well how to attribute correctly (ὀρθῶς) both the *timé* and the *atimíai*.

At the end of Book IV, Plato says that only that person who has a clean soul and is *agathos* is able to honour (*timan*) the Gods with sacrifices, wishes, *anathemata* (ἀναθήματα) and so on. And in the discussion about the soul,[95] Plato offers the deepest and most substantial account of the *timé* one ought to pay to his soul. The person who really honours his soul is not the one who offers presents to his soul, but the one who works for its improvement, aiming for its *anypsosis* (ἀνύψωσις). Similarly, Plato thinks that the Gods are not honoured by those who make sacrifices for them, but by those who are really *eulabes* (courteous), *osios* (holly), and *eusebes* (pious), and, above all, honour their souls. *Timé* must be paid only by those who intend to improve themselves. They, above all, ought to model themselves on the divine power which is above them.

The body for Plato comes third, after the Gods and the soul, but is worthy of *timé* as well.[96] However, man must understand that his body belongs to his soul and is no more than a tool of the latter. In understanding the above view, man will avoid on the one hand the adoration and deification of his body, and on the other the contempt and neglect of it.

Plato argues that the legislator must make sure that honours towards the young are paid as well. Such a man ought to advise the elders that they should respect the young'. What is worth noting here is that Plato changes the order of the old ethical demand 'respect the old' to 'respect the young. Respect and *timé* ought to be paid not to the old but to the young.

Finally, *timé* towards friends and foreigners is conceived by Plato as similar to those of the Greek tradition. Thus, a Magnesian citizen would be regarded as good if he could combine harmoniously the *thymoeides* and the *praon*, loving what is noble and good and not what is wicked and unjust, whilst paying *timé* both to the Gods, his soul and his body and avoiding self-love. These are the qualities Plato wants the new citizen of Magnesia to have in order to be *agathos* and contribute to the *eudaimonia* of his state as a whole. Indeed, Plato thinks

---

[94] Plato, *Laws*, 727a.
[95] Ibid., V 726a, 728d.
[96] Ibid., 728d.

that it is the task of *paideia* that will enable the soul to resist the violent downward pulls of pleasure and pain, boldness and fear. Once the soul has learnt to resist these, it will win the best victory over itself.

As we have already seen, Plato thinks this victory can be won in childhood if the love and desires of children are guided in a proper way through play. Indeed, if their play or even a drinking party is guided in a way that will lead children to acquire good habits, then *paideia* may succeed in directing them to virtue and their souls towards the proper objects of love. Therefore, Plato does not exclude pleasure from the Magnesian citizen's life. What he excludes is excesses of pleasure, and what he includes is proper and true pleasures, pleasures that the good legislator will allow because they will help the citizens to become moderate, courageous and good in every way.

It is the legislator–philosophers' task it is to distinguish between proper and improper pleasures and to make sure that there are laws against those who misuse true pleasures. Wine, for instance, Plato thinks is a gift of Dionysus and ought to be received into any state for its benefits. It is a gift that '…was intended to be a medicine and to produce reverence in the soul, and health and strength to the body'.[97] However if people do not receive the amount they ought to, but exceed it, it will no longer be a true pleasure and will drive people insane. Thus, the legislators must make sure that people receive the right amount of true pleasure. Part of their job is therefore to fix the right amount of any pleasure that is to be allowed in Magnesia where pleasure, though not a sufficient condition of the best life, and still thought to be in a lower place than that of knowledge, is nevertheless allowed. However, its allowance in Magnesia must be based on regulations made by the *logos* of the philosopher–legislators whose approximate use of *logos* confirms their state of mental health.

Plato and Philosophy

In the *Republic*, Plato distinguishes the philosopher from the lovers or sights and sounds.

> I set apart and distinguish those of whom you were just speaking, the lovers of spectacles and the arts, and men of action, and separate from them again those with whom our argument is concerned and who alone deserve, the appellation of philosophers or lovers of wisdom.

---

[97] Plato, *Laws*, 672.

He goes on to say that:

> the lovers of sounds and sights delight in beautiful tones and colours and shapes and in everything that art fashions out of these, but their thought is incapable of apprehending and taking delight in the nature of the beautiful in itself.[98]

However, this Platonic distinction raises a number of questions. What is the cause that moves the human soul to proceed to an examination of where reality is to be found in the world? What is the best way to base his theoretical research in order to reveal the depth of the substance of being? What are the areas of reality the philosopher will be concerned with? What will the results of his philosophic inquiries be?

As for the cause that forces the human soul to philosophise, Plato tells us in *Theaetetus*[99] that '...the sense of wonder (*thaumazein*) is the mark of the philosopher', whereas in the *Republic* he describes the natural dowry of the philosopher as '...by nature of good memory, quick apprehension, magnificent, gracious, friendly, and akin to truth, justice, bravery and sobriety'.[100]

The move of man towards philosophy takes place when he understands the limits of his humanity in the sense that some lines in his life cannot be grasped given that men do not have the power either to understand or to explain everything in the world. In a way, man, for Plato, is led towards philosophy because he appreciates both the insufficiency and deficiency of human knowledge. In the *Apology*, Plato portrays Socrates as having grasped this truth: 'The wisest of you men is he who has realised, like Socrates, that in respect of wisdom he is really worthless.'[101] Moreover, man, according to Plato, should not even have the right to claim that he possesses wisdom. The possession of wisdom is the privilege of God only, and not of man. What is possible for man, within the limits of his humanity, is his search for wisdom and the willingness he must have in order to become a friend and lover of wisdom. The soul of the philosopher is filled with a strong *eros* aiming to arrive as close a possible to the *on*. In the *Symposium*, Plato has described the motive that makes man's soul more towards a higher level of reality. He tells us that none of the Gods philosophise, as every God is wise. On the contrary, man's soul needs to philosophise, and only the man who is ignorant lives his life with the

---

[98] Plato, *Republic*, 476a–b.
[99] Plato, *Theaetetus*, 155d; Aristotle, *Metaphysics*, I 2, 982b.
[100] Plato, *Republic*, 487a.
[101] Plato, *Apology*, 23b.

illusion that he possesses *sophia*. Plato parallels man and *eros* in that they are both somewhere between wisdom and ignorance, perfection and imperfection.

Eros, for Plato, is '...gallant, impetuous and energetic, a mighty hunter, and a master of device and artifice – at once desirous and full of wisdom, a lifelong seeker after truth, an adopt in sorcery, enchantment and seduction'.[102]

Man's soul, Plato believes, has an erotic relationship with the philosophical life, that is also seen as erotic by Plato; it is gradually directed by its internal sentiment to admire the beauty of the world of ideas. From the time that man's soul faces the 'light' that is reflected by the ideas, it will start to feel an irresistible attraction towards them. This endeavour of the human soul to reach the realm of ideas signifies ontological perfection for that soul. For Plato, philosophy is a continuous search for the truth, and this is why in the Platonic dialogues there is never any announcement of finding knowledge. There are urges that make man's soul search for the truth.

Indeed, when man's soul comes close to the world of ideas, it comes close to the world of *theion* and thus the Platonic philosophy has an undoubtedly religious tone.

Philosophy, for Plato, has dialectic as its main instrument and basic method, whilst its subject is anything concerned with the nature, existence and purpose of man, and his relation to God or Gods. Thus, Plato in the *Phaedrus*[103] makes Socrates state that he himself 'cannot as yet know himself as the inscription of Delphi enjoins, and so long as that ignorance remains it seems to me ridiculous to inquire into extraneous matters'.

Socrates regards such theories as 'attractive, but as the invention of clever, industrious people who are not exactly to be envied, for the simple reason that they must then go on and tell us the real truth about the appearance of centaurs and the chimera.'

Dialectic with Plato is transformed into a power, whilst declaring that, 'The cognition of that which exists in reality, ever unchanged, is held, I cannot doubt, by all people who have the smallest endowment of reason to be far and away truer than any other'.[104]

In *Philebus* also, Plato characterises dialectic as a gift of the Gods, that indeed reaches mankind through Prometheus together with a fire exceeding bright.[105] As for the exercise of dialectic, Plato indeed emphasises that it is a

---

[102] Plato, *Symposium*, 203d.
[103] Plato, *Phaedrus*, 229d–e, 230a.
[104] Plato, *Philebus*, 58a.
[105] Ibid., 16c.

skill that only the philosopher is able to exercise. 'And the only person I imagine, to whom you would allow this mastery of dialectic is the pure and rightful lover of wisdom.'[106] The dialectician, Plato tells us, is able to distinguish the various faces of the real world and to connect them into a unified whole without forgetting their differences.

I believe it is worth noting here that Aristotle also, whilst despairing of finding a solid solution to this Platonic problem concerned with a clear distinction between *doxa* (opinion) and *episteme* (science), concluded that the only difference between philosopher and Sophist lies *in proairesis* (predisposition). 'For Sophistry and dialectic are concerned with the same class of subjects as philosophy, but philosophy differs from the former in the nature of its capability and from the latter in its outlook on life.'[107]

A similar point of view is expressed by J. Habermas when he writes that '...the truth of statements is linked in the last analysis to the intention of the good and the true life'.[108]

Philosophy, for Plato, can bring man close to God: 'That is why we should make all speed to take flight from this world to the other, and that means becoming like the divine so far as we can, and that again is to become righteous with the help of wisdom.'[109]

However, in spite of the fact that the philosopher lives where all ordinary men live, he differs from the latter in that only his body is actually placed together with those of the rest in the city, '...while his thought, disdaining all such things as worthless, takes wings, as Pindar says; beyond the sky, beneath the earth, searching the heavens and measuring the plains, everywhere seeking the true nature of everything as a whole never sinking to what lies close to hand'.[110] And '...anyone who gives his life to philosophy is open to such mockery. It is true that he is unaware what his next door neighbour is doing, hardly knows indeed whether the creature is a man at all; he spends all his pains on the question, what man is and what powers and properties distinguish such a nature from any other'.[111]

As the philosopher is different from other men, one of the aims of his life is to seek his own death, as only by dying will be able to free his soul. Evidently, in *Phaedo*, Plato states the role of philosophy to be preparation for

---

[106] Plato, *Philebus*, 253e.
[107] Aristotle, *Metaphysics*, IV, ii. 1004b 22–26.
[108] Habermas, 1971 (1968), p.317.
[109] Plato, *Theaetetus*, 176b.
[110] Ibid., 173d–e.
[111] Ibid., 174a.

death as Socrates is said to have understood and practised it.[112] Socrates is a philosopher, which implies fearlessness in the face of death and, indeed, practice of the latter during his life as his aim is to purify his soul.[113] This can be done only after his death because:

> It seems that so long as we are alive, we shall continue closest to knowledge if we avoid as much as we can all contact and association with the body, except when they are absolutely necessary and instead of allowing ourselves to become infected with its nature purify ourselves from it until God himself gives us deliverance. In this way by keeping ourselves uncontaminated by the follies of the body we shall probably reach the company of others like ourselves and gain direct knowledge of all that is pure and uncontaminated – that is, presumably of truth.[114]

Hence, the philosopher will only be able to reach reality, that Plato at the time sees as being constituted by 'the forms', after his death. The philosophy described as a study of death and a catharsis and purification of the human soul is treated as identical to ransom. In *Phaedo*,[115] Plato makes Socrates say that he is self-assured of the fact that the statesmen of Athens are neglecting to cultivate *sophrosyne and dikaiosyne* as he puts it in *Gorgias*. He tells us that, 'They have paid no heed to discipline and justice, but have filled our city with harbours and dockyards and walls and revenues and similar rubbish'.[116] This criticism is in total harmony with the conception of politics as a *techne* that is closely related to ethics and whose main mission is the cultivation and acquisition of *arete*.

In *Politicus*,[117] Plato tells us that the possessor of the 'science of kingship', whether he is in fact in power or has only the status of a private citizen, will property be called a 'statesman' since his knowledge of the art qualifies him for the title whatever his circumstances. For this reason, Plato writes in the *Republic* that the disastrous consequences of human life will end only when the philosophers become kings and vice versa. Indeed, in the *Republic* the role of philosophy is very emphatic in that it is very closely connected to good ruling, as the rulers of the *kallipolis* should be of a philosophic disposition. It could be

---

[112] Plato, *Phaedo*, 63b5–6, 69e3–5.
[113] Ibid., 90d.
[114] Ibid., 67a.
[115] Ibid., 91a.
[116] Plato, *Gorgias*, 519a.
[117] Plato, *Politicus*, 259b.

said that in the *Republic*[118] he offers an answer to what had already been conceived in *Gorgias*, when he stated that the statesmen of his time could neither conceive nor fulfil the first and main purpose of politics. In the same dialogue, putting it into the mouth of Socrates,[119] he tells us that he himself was one of the few Athenians, if not the only one, who was aware of the political science and was exercising it accordingly. In *the Republic*, Plato takes up this idea of the relation between politics and philosophy, so that he requires that the philosopher–kings of the *kallipolis* also be philosophers.[120] It is indeed these philosopher–kings, as they have been termed by many in our century, who will distribute *dikaiosyne* by making every person 'perform one social service in the state for which his nature was best adapted'.[121] This is because philosophy, for Plato, is not simply the bloom in the flowering of history; it is not only the understanding of the existence of God or Gods that compose historical reality, but the *Promethean* discovery of the human race and philosophical questions which are concerned with the fulfilment of the individual's life both in the individual and collective sphere.

Philosophy is concerned with the psychical search for the *archen* or *archai* of the world and it is indeed this which distinguishes philosophy from the other sciences. Plato tells us of it that it is *ep arche anypotheton* as a distinguishing mark between philosophy and the science of geometry.[122] Similarly to the *kallipolis*, Magnesia in the *Laws* is not a place for Sophists, but a place where the latter are once again condemned whilst the last word of everything is to be found in the role of philosophy.[123] For Plato, philosophy is still important and it is to be found in the members of the Nocturnal Council. The Nocturnal Council is the city's head and its components, that is, the ten most 'perfected guardians' together with the *hiereis* aimed at the salvation of the city's regime and laws. It aims to guide all Magnesians with *phronesis* and *nous* according to God's measure.[124] The Nocturnal Council is an image of the harmony of the one, similar to the rulers of the *Republic* who may also be seen as an image of the form of the good which they have in their hearts.

Philosophy in the *Laws*, as in the *Republic*, should only be studied by the comparatively old, who have previously spent many years of their lives

---

[118] Plato, *Gorgias*, 519a.
[119] Ibid., 521d.
[120] Plato, *Republic*, 433d; Plato, *Phaedrus*, 266c.
[121] Plato, *Republic*, 433a.
[122] Ibid., 510b–c.
[123] Plato, *Laws*, 960b–c, 969b–c; Plato, *Republic*, 536d.
[124] Plato, *Laws*, 747b, 817e–820d, 961d.

studying abstract and formal disciplines. This is because Plato knows that philosophy makes one question what has been taken for granted and so would have destructive effects if studied by the young, who may have rejected old truths but, being inexperienced, would have nothing to replace them. But by studying arithmetic, geometry, astronomy and harmonics at an early age, they will start preparing themselves for the non-empirical and highly abstract reasoning that is required by the philosophers.[125]

The Laws signifies that Plato remained loyal to the mission of philosophy Socrates had established, from the beginning of his career until its very end, always showing an incredible interest in human society and always attempting to help the latter by considering '...what means betterment could be brought about not only in these matters but also in the government as a whole'. Indeed, this political goal concerned Plato during his life.[126]

Plato writes on the relation between philosophy and politics, 'until finally looking at all the states which now exist, I perceived that one and all they are all badly governed; for the state of their laws is such as to be almost incurable... the right philosophy I was compelled to declare that by it one is enable to discern all forms of justice both political and individual'.[127]

It is indeed this idea of the closeness of philosophy and politics and necessity that they should coincide that was behind Plato's mind in his political works, the *Republic* and the *Laws*.[128] A distinctive basic characteristic of Plato's political philosophy is the idea that society should always be governed by the best, and by the best he means the true philosophers, that is, these men who are excellent naturally and can therefore provide antidotes to the problems of political societies by mixing morality and politics with philosophy.

The Nocturnal Council of the *Laws* is composed of such self-governing men who are educated and were ready to be educated further and whose task it is to help all those men who cannot reach 'true' standards in their life and have instead manufactured false ones, how to gain back their *autarkeia* (self-sufficiency). Thus, the role of the *philosopher-nomophylakes* is to lead men from false standards to true ones, as they are aware of the grievous errors to which ordinary men are prone; Plato's point, however, is that they can be corrected by reasonable discussion. In this way, philosophy will 'clear the dust' of the sceptics and the atheists, putting aside erroneous beliefs whilst showing that

---

[125] Plato, *Republic*, 521d–531c.
[126] Plato, *Epistle* VII, 325e, 326a.
[127] Ibid., 326a.
[128] Plato, *Republic*, 473, 326a–b.

the views to be adopted would be those of reasonable men who had not been confused and corrupted by the sceptics.

Thus, Plato wants his audience to discover reason for themselves. He aims at showing that true philosophy must be each man's discovery within himself; to make this discovery we must first know our true selves. The members of the Nocturnal Council, like the philosopher–kings of the *Republic*, are certainly reasonable men who knew themselves, and as such they could overturn false and erroneous beliefs correcting confusions. This is not to say, of course, that Magnesia is exactly like the *kallipolis*, as the latter is based on the unfettered discretion of the philosopher–kings and the former on written laws. Nevertheless, they have something in common, as do all Platonic dialogues – that is, the importance of the role of philosophy as a mirror of the self and as concerned with *sophia and phronesis*. Above all, they are attempts to show that the purpose of the state and its legislation is not the preservation and promotion of a single *arete*, like courage or bravery, for instance, but of *arete* as a whole. And it is this idea that the true *nomophylakes* of the state of the *Laws* must know, in order to be able to 'be genuine guardians of the laws they must have genuine knowledge of their real nature; they must be articulate enough to explain the real difference between good actions and bad and capable of sticking to the distinction in practice'.[129] In this way they will be able to educate and lead the citizens towards *arete* both with their reason and actions. They will be the means of *logos* and the *theosebeis* (religious) representatives of the belief in the divine authority, the immortality of the soul, in God's harmonious and orderly world, where Magnesia will only be an imitation of its goodness and perfection and human law the earthly expression of the divine *nous*.

---

[129] Plato, *Laws*, XII 966b.

Chapter IV

Introduction

Since ancient times there has been a line of thought that although Greece was the country where culture and philosophy were born and cultivated, when it came to *dikaion* and the development of jurisprudence in particular, Greece was very limited. This view is most evidently expressed by Cicero[1] in his attempt to make a comparison between the laws of Lycurgus, Draco and Solon, and those of the Roman *ius*. He concludes that the former were unsystematic and almost ridiculous (*inconditum ac paene ridiculum*). However, according to G. Glotz,[2] this view was disrespectful, because although the Roman *ius* was apparently better in the technical sense and more consistent than the *dikaion* of the ancient Greeks, the Athenian notion of justice had come into existence before that of the Romans. More importantly, the Athenian *dikaion* was the first notion of justice that involved the welfare of all citizens, whilst being unquestionably more flexible and more humane than that of the Romans. It was not merely theoretical, it was also practical.

In Greece, as Plutarch tells us, the emphasis was placed on practice, and the laws proposed had to be adapted to the existing conditions rather than the latter to the former. Indeed, Solon fitted his laws to the state of things, making things to suit his laws.[3] In this way, the interests of individuals were effectively protected and that is why it could be appropriate to say that the ancient Greek *dikaion* was superior to the Roman, as was more flexible in applying theory to practice and was more humane. As an example, we may consider the fact that in Roman law the *pater familias* was an absolute ruler, that is, he had complete authority over his *domus* (household) having the right of life and death over his children. The Greeks, on the other hand, conceived of the father as somebody who gave affection to his children whilst directing them in childhood.[4] The

---

[1] Cicero, *De Oratore*, I, 197.
[2] Glotz, 1904, III, p.1.
[3] Plutarch, *Lives*, vol. 1, Solon, 22, 3.
[4] Biscardi, 1982, p.101 ff.

same concern for individual interests could also be found in the attitude to items of real estate that had come from the wife's dowry. In contrast to other legislators, who considered the husband as the exclusive master of the wife's dowry, the Greek legislators thought the dowry belonged only to the wife. However, the fact that the Greeks were more flexible in practice did not mean they neglected theory. It is true to say that the contribution of the Greeks to the general theory of *dikaion* was substantial.

To justify my view about the origins and development of *dikaion* and jurisprudence, I recommend the reader to study the *peri dikaiou* or the *Republic* and the *peri nomon* or the *Laws* of Plato, as well as the teachings of Aristotle about the necessity of law and his theory of justice.

By approaching it in this way, the reader will discover that the origins and gradual development *of dikaion* and jurisprudence were to be found in Greece. He will thus allow himself to conceive of Greek law and legal theory as different from that of the Romans, but under no circumstances inferior.

The citizen of Athens, and possibly of other Greek states that also had a democratic form of government, participated equally in the exercise of political power in the *ekklesia*, and in the administration of justice in the law courts.[5] What is also worth noting is that the separation of powers into executive, legislative and judiciary was already known in Greek thought.[6]

The functions of what we now term legislative, executive and judiciary were all exercised by the *demos* as a whole. The *archon* organised the preparation of a lawsuit that was apparently divided into two stages comparable with the Roman division between the procedure 'in iure' and the 'apud judicem'. However, the magistrate in Rome was explicitly obliged to judge according to law. Under this system, the existence of individual members of the legal profession was not necessary as there were bodies of *dikasts* that were responsible for judging what really happened and for deciding the true meaning and implications of the laws.

In Athens, plaintiff and defendant had to plead their own case. Orators could and did act as *logographoi* (speech writers) but were not paid advocates. In Rome, legal advocacy was a profession, the courts were composed solely of members of the aristocracy, and orators like Cicero would take on cases and prosecute or defend in court. Presumably, this difference is part of what Cicero[7] is getting at in the *De Oratore*. He tells us that 'aque et apud Graecos

---

[5] Sinclair, 1988.
[6] Aristotle, *Politics*, IV 1297b37, 1298a3.
[7] Cicero, *De Oratore*, I, 45, 198. See also Finley, 1984, pp.30–1.

infimi homines mercedula adducti ministros se praebeunt in iudiciis oratoribus, ei qui apud illos (πραγματικοί) vocantur'. At this point it is essential to stress that, as is known from history, most of those who taught the greatest Roman teachers of legal science were either Greek or of Greek origin.

Thus, I believe that Cicero's criticism can be overthrown if we simply consider the tradition that, during the composition of the Twelve Tables, the Romans sent ambassadors to Athens in order to study and eventually to take the Athenian laws as their prime example. Indeed, these laws were the laws of Draco and Solon that Cicero seems to find ridiculous. In his criticism of the Athenian laws, he neglects to consider a basic fact that it was through the philosophy of Plato, Aristotle and Theophrastus among others that *dikaion*, *dikaiosyne and nomoi* had a theoretical analysis. Possible explanations for the harsh and unfair view of Cicero could be the fact that, in contrast to Rome, there was neither a single nor a unified *dikaion* in ancient Greece, possibly due to the geographical and political division of the Greek world, or it could just be his own haughtiness. It is true that even the notion of *ethnos* did not exist in Greece. In ancient times, the word *ethnos* had a very humble meaning, both for a group of people and for a group of animals. Yet I am aware that Herodotus[8] makes use of the term *Hellenikon ethnos* but in doing so he does not mean the totality of the Greeks, but simply the Dorians. He calls the Ionians *Pelasgikon ethnos*. 'The Lacedaemonians were the most eminent of the Dorian peoples and the Athenians of the Ionian. These two, one originally Pelasgian, the other Hellenic, were the most powerful of the Greek peoples.'

Theophrastus can be used as a source here, as he tells us of the divisions in the Greek world:

> I have often marvelled, when I have given the matter my attention, and it may be I shall never cease to marvel, why it has come about that, albeit the whole of Greece lies in the same clime and all Greeks have a like upbringing, we have not the same constitution of character.[9]

Thucydides also tells us that the differences between Sparta and Athens for instance had become even stronger.

> An Athenian is always an innovator, quick to form a resolution and quick at carrying it out. You, on the other hand, are good at keeping

---

[8] Herodotus, A, 56.
[9] Theophrastus, *Characters*, Letter dedicatory, 1.

things as they are; you never originate an idea, and your action tends to stop short of its aim... But your nature is always to do less than you could have done, to mistrust your own judgement... of them alone it may be said that they possess a thing almost as soon as they have begun to desire it... Their view of a holiday is to do what needs doing; they prefer hardship and activity to peace and quiet. In a word, they are by nature incapable either of living a quiet life themselves or of allowing anyone else to do so.[10]

Thus, as each Greek *polis* had its own political system and organisation, it would be rather an impossibility to put them together to form a unity. This is not to say, of course, that common customs and laws were not to be found in the *dikaia* of ancient Greece.[11] However, the fact that there might have been common laws was not sufficient to promote the unity of Greek *dikaion*. Even when there are common customs and laws we can notice a different approach and use of them in different cities.

Yet, the fact that there was no unity of *dikaion* in ancient Greece does not mean that there were not *ennomoi taxeis* (legal classes) in the Greek *poleis*.[12] In short, the ancient Greeks constructed something different from that which was previously current in the ancient world. For the first time, *nomos* (law) became accessible and was intended to form a part of the life of all Greek citizens, regardless of the number of those who had the control of laws in their hands. What was important in ancient Greece was that the law remained the ideal of all citizens.[13] The continuing misunderstanding of the contribution of the Greeks is due to our failure to examine closely the wealth of ancient Greek discussion *peri nomon*.

Until recently, it was thought that the *Laws* of Plato consists of a mere theoretical construction for a second Platonic ideal state. However, research on the subject has now shown that the *Laws* contains a 'treasury' of ancient Greek legal canons and customs.[14] Above all, it contains the first systematic treatment and exposition of jurisprudence. It shows that Plato was the first to have realised the necessity for the cultivation of jurisprudence. Although he still holds an ethical conception of *dikaiosyne* in the *Laws*, he presupposes the

---

[10] Thucydides, A, 70; See also Powell, 1985, pp.94–135, 214–262.
[11] See Thucydides, A, 41, T 58, 3, Δ 97, 2; Herodotus, H 144; Isocrates, VII 39.
[12] Finley, 1966.
[13] Aristotle, *Rhetoric*, 1373b3 19 ff.; Aristotle, *Politics*, 1289 A 20.
[14] Andrews, 1986, p.201.

internal belief of men in *dikaion* (justice).[15] In the *Laws* he goes further than in the *Republic*, and combines this with a legal conception of *dikaiosyne* (justice) that implies the obedience of the individual to the *Laws*, usually due to a fear of penalties. In the *Laws*, Plato works out the implications of the rule of law in a systematic way, recognising the need for legal institutions. He understands why the rule of law requires the provision of an executive of magistrates, a system of courts and a body of members of the judiciary. The latter are given the responsibility to apply these laws effectively and thus strengthen the legal system of the city to be founded. However, as Plato's conception of *dikaiosyne* does not restrict itself to the ethical sense only, he places emphasis on the legal restraints that should be imposed on the officials on the personal authority of both the magistrates and the *dikasts*, for it is law that is of divine origin not those who rule.

He goes on to say that it is the organisation of the *dikasteria* that is wholly responsible for the just distribution of *dikaiosyne*, considering that '...any state without duly established courts simply ceases to be a state'.[16] This view is both in contrast to that of the *Republic*, where the *kallipolis* is to be governed by the unfettered discretion of the philosopher–kings, and similar to the view of Aristotle. The latter also emphasised that *dikaiosyne* depends on the way it is exercised and awarded:

> ...how actions are to be performed and distributions made in order to be just – to know that there is a harder task than to know what one's health requires; because in medicine too, although it is easy to know what honey and wine and hellebore and cautery and surgery are, to know how and to whom and when they should be applied to produce health is no less a task than to be a qualified doctor.

Evidently, this is a more difficult thing than simply to know what is useful and beneficial for our health.[17]

In the *Laws*, Plato first of all distinguishes the *dikasteria* (courts) into *idion* (private) and *demosion* (public) and the disputes between people into private and public:

---

[15] Plato, *Republic*, 361.
[16] Plato, *Laws*, 766d 4–5.
[17] Aristotle, *Nicomachean Ethnics*, 1137a 15–16.

Cases may be brought before the other courts for two reasons: one private person may charge another with having done him wrong, and bring him to court so that the issue can be decided; or someone may believe that one of the citizens is acting against the public interests, and wish to come to the community's assistance.[18]

In other words, in the *Laws* Plato is telling us that there must exist two kinds of law courts. One of them is the *idion* for when an individual feels that he has been treated unjustly by another and wants to find justice; the other is the *demosion*, for when an individual feels that another has done wrong to the public interest, which he wants to defend.

Plato understands that there are many cities that have a great number of worthless legal provisions which are nevertheless the products of distinguished men. Thus, the *nomophylakes* of any state must choose, recalculate and reshape the existing provisions in such a way as to form the right legislation. This idea is evident in the *Laws*, where Plato stresses the importance of the Nocturnal Council in having the right to abandon, adopt, modify and recalculate existing institutions and laws, whilst also creating new ones in the hope of formulating a concrete and detailed scheme of political, legal and administrative justice for his law-governed state, Magnesia.[19]

However, in order to help the reader better appreciate Plato's contribution to both the ancient theory of justice and law and legal institutions, I feel the need to go back to earlier conceptions *of dike and dikaiosyne*, starting from Homer. Hence my next section.

Dike, *Dikaion* and *Dikaiosyne* from Homer to the Sophists
'The Old Stories Contain Elements of Truth'[20]

(a)   Homer and Hesiod

Chronologically, the first general statements we have on *dike and dikaion* are to be found in Hesiod:[21]

> The road to justice is the better way, for justice in the end will win the race... When justice is dragged out of the way by men who judge dishonestly and swallow bribes, a struggling sound is heard... But when

---
[18] Plato, *Laws*, 767b5–9.
[19] Ibid., 957a5, 957b4.
[20] Ibid., III 677a.
[21] Hesiod, *Works and Days*, 217, 226.

the judges of a town are fair, to foreigner and citizen alike, their city prospers and her people bloom.

What the verses mentioned above mean is that *dike* was thought at different times to be both a corrupting procedure and yet a fair one. *Dikaion* implied *arete*, and the latter was found in the *agathos* (man). The *themistes* having the right to administer *dikaion* are sometimes said to adopt the idea of the right justice, and at other times are thought to step on it. However Hesiod's description of those administering *dikaiosyne* as not always being in harmony with the idea of right *dikaion*, apparently did not have dramatic consequences on the consciousness of weak men, in the sense of leading them to a state of mistrusting and so disobeying them. My view can be justified, I believe, if we consider the following passages of the 62nd and 63rd Orphic hymns respectively.[22]

> 'For whatever base men consider matters that cannot be put
> to trial easily, unjustly wishing more than is fair,
> you intervene and rouse justice against the unjust.
> An enemy to the unjust, you are a gentle companion of
> the just'

> 'You rejoice in peace and you strive for a life that is stable.
> You loathe unfairness but fairness delights you,
> and in you knowledge of virtue reaches its noble goal.'

The passages of the 62nd and 63rd Orphic hymns make two points:

First, there is the idea that injustice is to be found in human selfishness, the cause of the shattering of men's equality in their attempt to proceed and reach the true good in life.

Second, we may see that this unjust breaking of order is quite unacceptable. It is also clear that the punishments imposed on offenders against the laws are wholeheartedly and unquestionably accepted. Indeed, the fight between *arete* (excellence) and *dikaiosyne* (justice) on the one hand, and *hybris* and injustice on the other, had always been the concern of the ancient Greeks, both the

---

[22] Orphic hymns 62–63. See also, *The Orphic Hymns*, Text and Translation. A. Athanasakis 1988, Scholars Press USA.

everyday men and the epic poets, tragedians and philosophers. It was the refutation of injustice that Homer portrayed in the *Iliad*.[23]

Similarly, Hesiod treats *dikaiosyne* as identical to *themistes* (judgements) with which the members of the judiciary are inspired directly from the Gods.

> Yet the men who in the name of Zeus safeguard our laws, the judges of our nation, hold it in their hands. By this I swear that the day is coming when the Achaeans one and all will miss me sorely, and you in your despair will be powerless to help them as they fall in their hundreds to Hector killer of men. Then, you will tear your heart out in remorse for having treated the best man in the expedition with contempt.[24]

> And let our judge be Zeus whose laws are just.[25]

Those who did not obey the laws were punished, since the Gods honoured *dikaion* and good deeds: 'What a lamentable thing it is that men should blame the Gods and regard us as the source of their troubles, when it is their own wickedness that brings them sufferings worse than any which Destiny allots them.'[26]

The Goddess Athena also advises Telemachus not to take into consideration the opinions of the suitors, as they were far from being just: 'So forget the suitors now and dismiss their plots and machinations from your mind. They are fools, and there is no sense or honour in them. Nor have they any inkling of the dark Fate that is stalking so near and will strike them all down in a single day.'[27] In the *Odyssey*, we are told that the land of the Cyclops is *athemistes* and unjust, as the Cyclops are described as neither knowing laws nor having any order.[28]

The concept of a *dikaiosyne* in both Homeric poems is bound up and equated with punishment or, more precisely, vengeance – and treated as identical to unwritten law.[29] The notion of vengeance threads through the *Iliad* as part of the essential plot, right from the opening offence of Agamemnon kidnapping Apollo's priestess, Chryseis, for which Apollo takes his revenge.

---

[23] Homer, *Iliad*, II 384–388.
[24] Ibid., A 237–239.
[25] Hesiod, *Works and Days*, 36.
[26] Homer, *Odyssey*, A 30 ff.
[27] Ibid., B 282.
[28] Ibid., A 112.
[29] Homer, *Iliad*, VI 35–65. See also the Bible, Leviticus 24:17–22, Matthew 5:38–41.

Indeed, the whole Trojan War is vengeance for Paris' abduction of Helen. However, alongside the conception of vengeance, as already noted above, Homeric society conceives of a customary conduct reinforced partly by the *dikai* (judgements) and *themistes* (layings down) delivered by the *gerontes* (elders), *diotrepheis basileës* (kings guided by the Gods) and *dikaspolois*, and partly by direct communal action. As an example, I would give the *dike* about the Shield of Achilles in the *Iliad*.[30]

Yet in the *Odyssey*, this was not the only way of administering justice. There was also another way of settling the differences between people: by fighting[31] and without excluding the possibility of reaching a compromise between them.[32] In circumstances where someone felt he had to take a case to a third party, the latter normally being the kings. Homer mentions in the *Odyssey*[33] that Nestor was thought to be the most experienced in administering justice, having been king for three generations.

In the *Iliad*,[34] it is said that Zeus offered the laws of justice to the kings. The kings, whilst expressing their decisions, took into consideration the views of the public, regardless of the fact that the latter did not participate in them. It was according to this principle that the unwritten law was accepted by the masses in the Homeric period,[35] when the *dikasts*, like the legislators, were the instruments of God and the judicial decisions pronounced were either thought to have been inspired by Zeus or to have come directly from Zeus.

As Cicero writes[36] 'Quod autem non iudex, sed deus ipse rindex constituitur praesentis poenae metu religio confirmani ridetur'. Thus, *dikaiosyne* in the Homeric period was viewed as *ek Dios themistes* (divine judgements) and *theon nomima* (divine laws). When the power of the kings to administer justice became political, the latter was gathered solely in their hands, but after the abolition of kingship, this power passed to the nobles. Now, the judicial functions were exercised on the basis of the nobles' absolute and uncontrolled views. For this reason, their judicial decisions were often thought to be unjust.

> When justice is dragged out of the way by men who judge dishonestly and swallow bribes, a struggling sound is heard; then she returns back

---

[30] Homer, *Iliad*, IH 497–508.
[31] Homer, *Odyssey* E 470–3; Homer, *Iliad*, M 421–424.
[32] Homer, *Iliad*, I 632–636.
[33] Homer, *Odyssey*, T 244–245.
[34] Homer, *Iliad*, B 205–6, 9, 298–299.
[35] Aristotle, *Rhetoric*, 1468b, 7, 13, 1373 b, 4.
[36] Cicero, *De Legibus*, II 10, 35.

to the city and the homes of men wrapped in a mist and weeping, and she brings harm to the crooked men who drove her out.[37]

All people look to him when he is giving judgement uprightly, And speaking with assurance, he can stop great quarrels sensibly.[38]

During that period, the unjust and wrong *themistes* offered by those exercising the judicial function in the state were often thought to be the products of bribery.[39]

At this point, I ought to mention that I am aware that the suggestion of Hesiod has often been doubted. It has been suggested that in the time of Hesiod, judicial decisions were taken by the kings, but only after the latter had discussed them publicly in the *agora*.

According to Diodorus,[40] in *Thespies*, which seems to be the basis of Hesiod's poems, there was a collective kingship. It could have been that Hesiod was moved to describe the judicial circumstances of his time in a rather tragic way for personal reasons.[41] This could also explain why Hesiod's description of the local *archons*, who decided in favour of his brother Perses as '*dorophagous*', did not affect even the minds of the weak men.

However, in my view, Hesiod lived in the period when it became obvious that the *themistes*, *made* by those in power, were contrary to those made by the *gerantes diotrepheis basileës* or *dikaspoloi* of the Homeric period, that were believed to have been inspired directly from Gods.

(b) Nature and Convention: the Presocratics and the Sophists

The conception that *dikaiosyne* expresses the *theon nomima* contains the first 'seeds' of the theory about the *physei dikaion*. It is worth stressing that this view disconnects the perfection of the law and the distribution of justice from human will, as the latter is thought to aim at satisfying individual, and often unstable, intentions. Thus, it is thought that above the characteristic of men such as selfishness, there must exist as precious, rare and inexorable perfection of law. Indeed, the Presocratic philosophers very quickly, found this perfec-

---

[37] Hesiod, *Works and Days*, 221–225.
[38] Hesiod, *Theogony*, 84–86.
[39] Hesiod, *Works and Days*, 38–39, 219–221, 264.
[40] Diodorus, *Thespies*, D 29, 4.
[41] See Gagarin, 1974, pp.103–111; Bernardete, 1967, pp.150–177 29; West 1978.

tion of law in nature. This idea of cosmic *dikaiosyne* is expressed in a passage from Anaximander that Simplikios preserved.[42]

What Anaximander seems to express is that there will be some analogy between air, fire, earth and water in the world. Every divine element tends to try to extend its *kratos*. However, there is an element of necessity or *physei nomos* that restores their balance. In this way, *dikaiosyne* is what makes certain that there will be no excesses of any particular element in the world.

Apparently, it is this general conviction of the *physei dikaion* that we may find in Heraclitus, as Plutarch tells us of him.

This inexplicable perfection of law in cases where the harmony was broken through injustice was to be found even in the Olympian Gods; they were also thought to have both human *arete* and human weaknesses. And, as in their *kratos* there was not harmony but anarchy, it was quite natural for some thinkers to hold that the Olympian Gods had to be erased from the minds of men since *dikaiosyne* for men was equivalent to harmony. It was this feeling that was conceived and expressed by the tragic poets and the philosophers.

Although Sophocles is not particularly critical of the Olympian Gods, his first tragedy, *Ajax*, poses the question of whether one should obey and respect a judicial decision regardless of its rightness or wrongness. He puts the answer in the mouth of Ajax: 'A foe's gifts are no gifts and profits are not – wherefore in future we must learn to bend before the Gods, and try to reverence the sons of Atreus'.[43]

In this tragedy, Sophocles takes the first step in raising a problem that is illustrated better in *Antigone*, that is, whether those who represent the law (in this case Agamemnon) have the right to prohibit the members of the family of a dead person from burying his corpse. The equivalent character in *Ajax*, rather than Sophocles, regards the *physei dikaion* as identical to the *theon nomoi* according to which no one is allowed to humiliate the *esthlos* (good, fine) when the latter dies.

In *Antigone*, a clear distinction is made between the laws of the Gods and the demands of the king in that a) the commands of the king do not have so much power as to allow them to overcome the unwritten and unmistaken laws of the immortals,[44] and b) that the canons of unwritten laws prevail over written ones.[45] The commentator on *Antigone* must also refer to another

---

[42] Kirk, Raven, Schofield, p.117.
[43] Sophocles, *Ajax* 666.
[44] Sophocles, *Antigone*, 454–455.
[45] Aristotle, *Rhetoric*, 1373 b 4–1.

tragedy of Sophocles that was inspired by the Theban cycle, *Oedipus the king*.[46] In the second *stasimon* of the tragedy, the chorus of Theban elders reprimands Jocasta for her disrespect towards the divine, demonstrating its belief in Gods and in their unwritten laws.[47]

Furthermore, the commentator concerned with the unwritten just laws of the Gods must consider *Electra*[48] in particular, where the Chorus says:

> ...but by Zeus' lightning and divine justice in the sky, trouble shall soon follow! O voice that for mortals travels below the earth, cry out a sad message to the Atreidae below, carrying a joyless message of dishonour![49]

In *Oedipus at Colonus*, one of the last works of Sophocles, the poet thinks of *aidos* and *dike*, placing them at the same level as Zeus. Thus, whereas he makes Polyneikes stress that 'Since Mercy shares the throne of Zeus with regard to all his actions, let her stand by you also, Father!', he makes Oedipus say that 'these curses overcome your supplication and your thrones, if Justice sits of old beside the throne of Zeus according to the ancient laws.' It is worth noting that Sophocles used the term *themis* in *Electra* whereas in *Antigone* and *Oedipus the King* he used the terms *dike* and *nomos*, implying unwritten *nomos*.

From the above it should be obvious to the reader that Sophocles takes a religious position about the *agraphoi nomoi* (unwritten laws) possibly due to the fact that he was living in a period where the citizen was a particle of the city and men were taught *dikaion* in the *agora*, respecting traditional myths and the poetic works of Homer and Hesiod. Hence, I believe Aristotle is right to characterise Sophocles as (an) Imitator of Homer[50] Aristotle goes on to say that 'If it be objected that the description is not true to fact, the poet may perhaps reply, "But the objects are as they ought to be": just as Sophocles said that he drew men as they ought to be; Euripides as they are'.[51]

---

[46] Sophocles, *Oedipus the King*, 863–872.

[47] May such a destiny abide with me, that I win praise for a reverent purity in all words and deeds sanctioned by laws that stand high, generated in lofty heaven, the laws whose only Father is Olympus! The mortal nature of men did not beget them; neither shall they eer belulled to sleep by forgetfulness. Great in these laws is the God, nor does he ever grow old.

[48] Sophocles, *Electra*, 1063–1065.

[49] Sophocles, *Oedipus at Colonus*, 1267–1268 and 1381–1382.

[50] Aristotle, *Poetics*, 1448a 30.

[51] Ibid., 1460b 39–40.

However, the Greek public of that period was starting to demand that written laws should be imposed: laws that would be known to everyone and could be applied to everyone. In this way, the Greeks would refuse two basic *aretai* that ought always to be found in *dikaion*.

First was the equal application of the law to everyone.[52] Second, written laws would make for far greater security in a man's exchange of goods and would strengthen his relations with his fellow citizens. It was exactly because of these ideas that the conception that *dikaion* was and must be the demands of law became supreme in that period. Moreover, a formal definition of law was also demanded. According to Xenophon, Alcibiades, an associate of both Critias and Socrates, has remarked to Pericles that no one deserves praise unless he knows what a law is. Pericles answers that laws are what is approved and enacted by the majority in assembly whereby the latter answer what ought and ought not to be done. Yet Pericles admits that if obedience is obtained by mere compulsion it is force and not law, even though the law is enacted by the sovereign power in the state.

Xenophon also reports an alleged conversation between Socrates and the sophist Hippias in which both maintains a link between law or what is lawful and justice or what is right, admitting that laws may be changed or annulled. Socrates claims that there are 'unwritten laws', uniformly observed in every country which cannot conceivably be products of human invention. These are made by the Gods for all men, and when men transgress them, nature penalises them. Indeed, this idea was a part of Athenian society of the fifth century BC. The citizens of Athens had already gone through a partial shift from a morality of deeds to a morality of intentions, a shift which had already found expression in their drama.

In *the Oresteia*[53] of Aeschylus, a morally avant-garde trilogy, we see a shift from the blood feud to the law court, from the old to new kind of justice. The emergence of the latter at the end of the play demands the existence of a judicial and political authority. The *Erinyes*, the Furies, insist on kin murder and then punish the murderer, regarding the punishment as a necessity to achieve a healthy society. However, Orestes is set free, in contrast to all the other members of the family who have already paid for the crimes they have committed. The Goddess Athena listens to Orestes explaining why he has murdered his mother. Orestes tells her that he will accept her decision whatever it is. This implies Orestes' respect of the Areopagus and its decisions,

---

[52] Euripides, *The Suppliant Women*, 429–437.
[53] Aeschylus, *The Oresteia, Eumenides*, 588 ff., 655 ff., 682 ff., 696 ff., 726 ff., 767, 1055.

showing his understanding that the last word of all is to be found in the courts and their *nomoi*. Thus, the *physei dikaion* has been to some extent replaced by *nomo dikaion*, with *dike* being a reflection of the latter and of *dikaiosyne* in general, and, indeed, necessary for the establishment of *eurythmia* (harmonious arrangement) in society.

Xenophon also tells us, '...but what disgrace is it to me if other people fail to decide or act rightly with regard to me? And I see also the reputation left behind them among later generations by men of earlier times is not the same for the doers as for the sufferers of wrong',[54] Aristotle asserts, 'But when a man takes more than his share, although he is often actuated by none (much less by all) of these vices, yet what actuates him is certainly some kind of wickedness: viz., injustice. Therefore there is another kind of injustice which is a part of the unjust in general which means contrary to the law'.[55]

However, very characteristic are the cynical views of justice expressed by the Sophists in the first century BC. The Sophists had long been concerned with the antithesis between nature and convention, and had attributed law to human invention, justifying obedience to the latter only to the extent that it promoted one's advantage. Some of them considered laws as contrary to nature and viewed man as an egoistically motivated antisocial being, in contrast to both Plato and Aristotle who thought of man as, by nature, a 'political animal' (*Zôon politikon*). The Sophists indeed dealt with notions of law, justice, religion, custom and morality *Zôon politikon* and attempted to formulate a great number of the crucial problems of legal philosophy whilst attempts were also made formally to define the law. However, some of them attempted to explain humanity without reference to the Gods, placing more emphasis on the power of man, whom Protagoras apparently considered to be 'the measure of all things'.

In *Gorgias*, Plato portrays Callicles[56] as holding that man is no exception to the law of nature, according to which the stronger rules; man-made laws and social institutions violate human nature. One needs to point out here the distinction between those who saw man-made laws as a hindrance to natural justice (Callicles and Thrasymachus), and those who see such laws as necessary for communal life and even beneficial (Protagoras and possibly Antiphon).

---

[54] Xenophon, *Memorabilia*, 12–13.
[55] Aristotle, *Nicomachean Ethics*, E 1129b 12.
[56] Plato, *Gorgias*.

In Callicles' view, law and justice were merely a device of the majority of weaklings to keep the strong man, who is nature's just man, from his rightful place. *Nomos and physis were* enemies, and *dikaion* was on the side of *physis*. Indeed, this attitude to the law represented by Callicles was common in the late fifth century BC, along with the belief that necessity forced men to combine for survival and that communal life is impossible without submission to the law.

Thrasymachus in *Republic I*,[57] could also serve as a relevant example here, as he also dismisses conventional views of justice and morality, arguing that right is the preserve of the stronger and of those who rule. The speeches of Thrasymachus and Callicles must have expressed sentiments currently existing in Athenian society. The same views are also mirrored in the dialogue between the Athenian ambassadors and the *archons* of Melos: believing in the superiority of Athens, the Athenian ambassadors simply demand that the Melians give in.[58]

This picture of the Athenians is somehow contrary to the idea that history offers us, that Athens was the city where *arete* (excellence) was cultivated. However, I believe it is this contradiction that Plato expresses so vividly in his *Republic* in order to show the difference between the reality of something, and the virtuous impressions we might have: 'Then since it is "the seeming", as the wise men show me, that "masters the reality" and is lord of happiness, to this I must devote myself without reserve'.[59]

Plato knows that there are people who hold the position taken up by Adeimantus that '...we shall say that it is not justice that you are praising but the semblance, nor injustice that you censure, but the seeming, and that you really are exhorting us to be unjust but conceal it, and that you are with Thrasymachus in the opinion that justice is the other man's good, the advantage of the stronger, and that injustice is advantageous and profitable to oneself but disadvantageous to the inferior'.[60] Above all, Plato is aware that *dikaiosyne* (justice) in his time is nothing more than the hypocrisy that covers and promotes the interests of the strong at the expense of the weak. Thus, one may wonder how Plato faced this bitter reality of his time, and how he himself conceived of *dikaiosyne* (justice).

---

[57] Plato, *Republic*, I 338e–339a.
[58] Thucydides, *History*, E 105, 2.
[59] Plato, *Republic*, 365c.
[60] Ibid., 367c.

Plato's Response: the Necessity for Justice, Jurisprudence and Medical Punishment

It is Socrates who sets out a theory of *dikaiosyne* (justice). In *Crito*,[61] as Plato portrays Socrates, telling us that *dikaiosyne* is an individual *arete*, sowing the first seeds of the idea that *dikaiosyne* is the expression of moral values and that '...goodness and integrity, institutions and laws are the most precious possessions of mankind', as '...justice means equal shares not excess and that it is more shameful to do than to suffer wrong'.[62] In this way comes, '...the best way of life – to live and die is in the pursuit of righteousness and all other virtues',[63] because only '...the man who has led a godly and righteous life departs after death to the Isles of the Blessed, and there lives in all happiness exempt from ill, but the godless and unrighteousness man departs to the prison of vengeance and punishment which they call Tartarus'.[64] In *Crito*, Socrates declares the necessity of law whilst refusing to evade execution on the grounds that this punishment has been decreed according to the laws of Athens. His argument is based on a kind of agreement between citizens and state to observe these laws, whatever the consequences may be to a particular individual. Hs own duty to the laws rests upon his own agreement with them: were he to break it, the state would be harmed. Individual interests, therefore, should be harmonised in the social interest, and so should the freedom of every individual.

It was this view of *dikaiosyne* as an individual *arete* that Socrates intends to illustrate. In order to justify it, he offers his own *ethos* of life and death.[65]

While this view is put in the mouth of Socrates, I take it as the result of Plato's general conception *of dikaiosyne* as a necessary phenomenon that leads successfully to giving each man his due so that the well-being of the community is to be found in its legislation and administration which ensure that *dikaiosyne* is administered correctly and justly. In that way, both legislation and administration were thought to lead to the harmony of social living, *eurythmia* as Plato puts it in *Protagoras:*[66] 'For rhythm and harmonious adjustment are essential to the whole of human life,' along with the preservation of all the

---

[61] Plato, *Gorgias*, 51a–52b.
[62] Ibid., 489a.
[63] Ibid., 527e.
[64] Ibid., 523a–b.
[65] Xenophon, *Memorabilia*, D IV 10.
[66] Plato, *Protagoras*, 326b.

values of the state. It is in *Protagoras*[67] that Socrates regards justice as '...either the same thing as holiness or very like it'. He goes on to say that '...justice unquestionably resembles holiness and holiness justice'. Absence of legislation implies destruction of the city. Both legislation and administration will exist as long as the community exists. Furthermore, it is true that the more developed a state, the more legislation and administration will be needed, as they both contribute to making the members of the state not only self-sufficient but also able to lead their lives towards their *telos*. Thus, Socrates finds that *dikaiosyne* is a necessity for self-presentation and the promotion of some interests, but he denies Thrasymachus' assertion that the main interests are those of the stronger.[68]

Thus, the question that arises naturally at this point is: 'whose interest does Socrates have in mind when he admits that the just is something that is of advantage?' For Socrates, the purpose of *dikaiosyne* is not to be in the interests of those who rule but in the interests of all those who are ruled. He tells us that '...neither does anyone in any office of rule in so far as he is a ruler consider and enjoin his own advantage but that of the one whom he rules and for whom he exercises his graft and he keeps his eyes fixed on that and on what is advantageous and suitable to that in all that he says and does',[69] in such a way that it becomes apparent that '...no art or office provides what is beneficial for itself – but as we said long ago it provides and enjoins what is beneficial to its subject, considering the advantage of that, the weaker, and not the advantage of the stronger'.[70] This is because injustice is the cause of 'hatreds and internecine conflicts' whereas 'justice brings oneness of mind and love'.[71] These ideas are contrary to those of Glaucon who holds that justice '...is accepted and approved, not as a real good, but as a thing honoured in the lack of rigour to do injustice'.[72] Glaucon goes on to say that '...a man would never make a compact with anybody neither to wrong nor to be wronged for he would be mad' and that, according to Aeschylus,[73] he who 'will have honours and gifts because of that esteem',[74] is also called just.

---

[67] Plato, *Protagoras*, 331b.
[68] Plato, *Republic*, 339b.
[69] Ibid., 342.
[70] Ibid., 359a–b.
[71] Ibid., 351d.
[72] Ibid., 359a–b.
[73] Aeschylus, *Seven Against Thebes*, 593.
[74] Plato, *Republic*, 361c.

However, in order to illustrate his answer about the goodness of justice more explicitly and justifiably to his interlocutors, Socrates tells us that, 'The origin of the city... is to be found in the fact that we do not severally suffice for our needs but each of us lacks many things'.[75] In the *polis*, man is the unique creature that forms the highest value to the extent that the *polis* does not aim solely at making its members self-sufficient (*autarkes*), but also able to fulfil their lives as real humans.

Aristotle also notes this double purpose of the state (in his *Politics*), stressing that, 'The final association, formed of several villages is the state. For all practical purposes the process is now complete; self-sufficiency has been reached and while the state came about as a means of securing life itself, it continues in being to secure the good life'.[76]

The 'ev zen' (living well) according to Aristotle, is recommended in *Zen* (living) according to *arete* because '...the association which is a state exists not for the purpose of living together but for the sake of noble actions'.[77]

Plato notes that the perfect foundation of the state is to be found in its having the following four virtues: wisdom, courage, temperance and justice. Wisdom is to be found in the guardians; courage in the auxiliaries; temperance in the harmony of the state as a whole and justice when each man in the state minds his own business and does one job without meddling in the affairs of others. As such, justice for Plato is seen as 'oikeiopragia (οικειοπραγια)[78] both in the state and in the individual soul. All three classes, the guardians, the auxiliaries and the artisans of the state, and the three elements, the rational, the spirited and the appetitive parts of the individual soul, must fulfil and not simply mind their own proper function, without trespassing on those of others. Justice, therefore, in the *Republic* is the health and harmony of both the soul and the state, whereas injustice represents the appetitive condition.[79]

In this merely theoretical definition of justice Plato has the philosophers ruling the city, taking the good itself, the good 'beyond being' as its *arche and telos*. In this way, he makes them responsible for the exclusion of all lawlessness (*paranomia*) from the souls of the young, through a proper *paideia* which implies the exclusion of all lawlessness from the state. Plato appears to make laws quite unnecessary though only in principle, because in practice there are frequent references to both laws and legislation (*nomos* and *nomothesia*). Laws

---

[75] Plato, *Republic*, 369b.
[76] Aristotle, *Politics*, 1252 b 27–30.
[77] Ibid., 1281 a, 2.
[78] Plato, *Republic*, 434c.
[79] Ibid., 441e.

are not absent from the *Republic* as many scholars, who have apparently misread the work, have thought.[80]

Although I appreciate that the laws of the *Republic* are ideal ones, in the same way as is Plato's whole notion of justice, the reason for Plato's idealism can easily be explained if we glance at the time and place when the *Republic* was written. It was written in the city of the glories of the Persian Wars, the Athenian empire, the Parthenon, theatre, tragedy, comedy, Socrates and the funeral speech of Pericles. However, Athens was no longer at the height of its glory. Plato had not lived during the epoch-making times that Athens had offered to mankind in the last hundred years. He was born four years after the start of the Peloponnesian War, which indeed marked a turning point in Greek history. He had grown up in a period when the established order was on the verge of dissolution under the pressure of political events and theoretical criticism from the Sophistic movement. The values of the state ceased to be instinctive and affirmative and the ambitions of the people had become full of 'arfivisme'. Demagogues were becoming more and more prominent, and the faith of the people a subject of rationalistic irony. Thus, Euripides in *The Trojan Women*, was forced to say through Hecuba that he did not know whether the being that holds the earth in his hands is 'Zens, whether inflexible law of nature or man's mind'.[81]

Nevertheless, the Greeks knew that they were particles of a city where justice was included in their *recline* of living. In the *Republic*, Plato attempts in a way to re-establish standards of thought and conduct for a civilisation that seemed to be in political chaos. However, in so doing he does not aim at establishing a new order of ideas and institutions with a demand for radical reconstruction, but rather to find an ideal balance between order and freedom, founded on an understanding of *phronesis*, to use the term in the Aristotelian sense. The conditions and the pattern Plato adopts for the *kallipolis* are ideal ones, and though laws do exist they are philosophical rather than practical. This is in contrast to his state in the *Laws*, where Plato is concerned with concrete reality and with the modification of actual laws to be laid down for governing an actual state, and combines theory with practice.

In the *Laws*, Plato takes up the indications of the truly just city concealed in the *Republic* and puts them into effect. The *Republic* is an imitation *(mimesis)* of the most beautiful and most excellent life *(kalliston* and *ariston bion)*. In the

---

[80] Plato, *Republic,* 427b (religion), 459e (festivals), 409e (practice of medicine), 471b (war), 468b (military honours), 453d–457 (private property), 417b (guardians).
[81] Euripides, *The Trojan Women*, 886.

Laws, Plato confirms the unrivalled value of the *ariste politeia* as the prototype.[82] He is now legislating for a state that would resist the historical reality of the time, but, unlike the *kallipolis*, would be based on the rule of law.

In the *Laws* he also recalls the ideas of the myth of *Politicus* where the beginning of *nomokratia* (the rule of the law) is apparently alluded to, and it is argued that a genuine commonwealth must be a mixed constitution and in a true civil society the supreme authority must be no man nor body of men but the law. However, the fact that Plato thinks of written laws so highly at this stage, does not mean that all existing systems were not flawed in some way or other. Plato does not mean that all laws are good, or at any rate equally good. Hence his criticism in the preliminary books of the *Laws* which shows that many laws could reasonably be suspected of serving ambition and wealth and, as it was defined by certain Sophists, expressing the interest of the ruling power in the state.[83] In this way, Plato would justify the idea already expressed in *Minos*,[84] that existing laws are flawed. The fact that not all laws are good justifies the idea of the mixed constitution which copies elements of the constitutions of all three states under discussion in these early books of the *Laws*.

When, at the end of Book III, Kleinias reveals that he is a member of a commission charged with making laws for a new Cretan city, Plato can use the history of Book III for his didactic purpose, so that he will shape the state correctly. In doing so he combines theory and practice and blends philosophical ideals with imperfect real historical facts, in order to help transform them into a scheme of the best possible constitution.

Two, the *Laws* shows that legal theory does not begin with Locke or Marx, as many scientists and political theorists have assumed in modern times, but with Plato. I also believe that if the *Republic* had been examined closely enough, it would have limited the fame of the German sociologist Max Weber

---

[82] Plato, *Laws*, 739c, 746b–c.

[83] Ibid., 890a.

[84] According to the traditional chronological order of the Platonic dialogues, *Minos* was written before the *Laws*. However, it has been disputed that *Minos* is authentic Plato. But if *Minos* is authentic, he then indeed raises the question: 'what is law?' which he then in the *Laws* backs up with his criticism of all the three states, Sparta, Crete and Athens, in the sense that he finds flaws in all of them. My interpretation here is based on an article 'On the *Minos*' by Leo Strauss from the book *The Roots of Political Philosophy*. (Ten forgotten Socratic dialogues translated with interpretative studies, edited by Thomas L. Pangle.)

The authenticity of the dialogue *Minos* has been doubted by: Boeckh, 1806; Heidel, 1896; Pavlu, 1910; Jaeger, 1960, p.319; Wilamowitz, 1929, p.659. See also Taylor, 1948.

for his theory of ideal types, as Plato had made the similar social distinctions twenty-two centuries before him.

Similarly, Jean-Jacques Rousseau, Thomas Hobbes and Hegel, who all brought the theory of a social contract to maturity,[85] were not actually the first to form the theory of a social contract in the history of political philosophy; it was Plato in the *Laws*, where we have a masterful combination of theory and practice – that is, a contract based on a concrete and realistic rather than abstract basis. Consequently, I look to the *Laws* rather than *Republic* II for a social contract theory.

In the *Laws* we have an account of how human life ought to be lived and why people should choose the proposed city of Magnesia. Above all, we have a justification of the importance of law which is seen here as the only instrument that would enable the Magnesians to control their city effectively and to preserve the city's well-being. Plato advises us that the way to learn about law would be to look at the actual systems of various states in operation. This Platonic idea had great echoes in Montesquieu's *De l'Esprit des lois* (The Spirit of the Laws),[86] where the philosopher attempts also to find how the state can acquire tranquillity and security, arguing that the latter can be achieved only when the constitution sets inviolable limits to the action of the state and where the law itself guarantees the rights of the individual. Moreover, respect for the law was the prevailing Greek attitude of the time. As Diogenes Laertius notes,[87] at the time of the *Laws* the Academy was widely recognised as a place where men were trained in legislation and were often called to make use of their profession. Thus, it may have been Plato's aim to make his interlocutors act as jurists as well as being educators, legislators and philosophers.

It is equally true that in the *Republic* Plato suggests to practising politicians the need to become philosophers in order to save Athens from the existing corruption in both social and political life. Yet I find it hard to believe that such a treatise could ever be put into force by such politicians. Plato is well aware, as he himself tells us, that the *Republic* is a fairy tale or fable about justice; because of its independence of place and time and of geography and history, it is intended to take place in heaven as Socrates once suggested.

With his realisation that the proposed scheme of the *kallipolis* to influence man was far removed from ordinary life, Plato set himself the task of composing a more comprehensive plan of human life in a non-utopian and not ideally

---

[85] This idea of a social contract became the central speculative doctrine of modern social and political philosophy in the seventeenth and eighteenth centuries, theory of nature.
[86] Montesquieu trans. Nugent, 1949.
[87] Diogenes Laertius, III 46.

just form, unlike that of the *Republic*. I suggest that Plato brought his political plan to its culmination with the theory of law and jurisprudence, through his appreciation of the fact that political philosophy dealing with man should be concentrated only on what human beings can do and nothing more, whilst justifying his view that the state is truly and superlatively natural. This implies that in a society without laws man will not be a man but something different. Being human, as Aristotle puts it later in his *Politics*, implies a difference between man and animals in the sense that man can reason whereas animals cannot. Indeed, Plato placed great importance on the use of reason even from the beginning of his writings, allowing the interlocutors of every dialogue to reason and thus understand the differences between appearance and reality; knowledge and belief, lawfulness and lawlessness and so on. The importance of reason in the *Republic* is in Plato's development of his theory of justice both in the state and in the soul.

In the *Laws*, Plato emphasises the importance of reason in his definition of law – 'Law is reasoned thought'[88] – embodied in the decrees of the state. However, he now combines reason with experience. Experience can be found both in the fact that the interlocutors are old men as well as in the Athenian's use of history. It is reason that tells them that to embark on a philosophico-political programme and that they must start with a small stock of ideas, concepts and laws already in force. This implies that none of the three existing states had laws that, if taken on their own, would contribute to the best political *ethos* for Magnesia.

Plato's critical view of existing states explains partly, I believe, why the *Laws* is not set in any actual state or indeed in Sicily, though certain clues suggest that at least the early books of the work were possibly composed during Plato's visit to the young Dionysius in Syracuse.[89]

I believe that it would be meaningless and pointless for anyone to determine how reliable Plato's prehistory is. It must be noted that in a similar way, philosophers like Hobbes and Rousseau presented their theories of the basis of society in an historical form but there is little real history there. Plato's concept is an expression of the traditional Greek views of their past, rather than what modern historians would recognise as secure facts.

Nevertheless, Plato does offer a reason why of the three Dorian kingdoms it was Sparta that was saved whereas Argos and Messene sank. Sparta is shown to have been fortunately preserved by the same division of power which Plato

---

[88] Plato, *Laws*, 835–836. See also Plato, *Laws*, 714c: '...this distribution of reason with the name of law'. Aristotle, *Nicomachean Ethics*, 1180a, 21.
[89] Plato, *Epistle* VII, 331c–332a.

will implement in Magnesia: a balance in the constitution and a division of the powers of sovereignty between several parties; concentration of power in the same hands is always fatal. In the absence of this internal division of sovereignty in states, there was no adequate check on the temptation, natural to the monarchs, to extend their prerogative.[90] Sparta is thus portrayed as having a mixed constitution and a government which is neither an extreme autocracy, nor an extreme democracy, but a mixture of the two. The division of power can be found in its dual kingship, the aristocratic *gerousia* and the popularly elected board of *ephors*, which all formed the secret of Sparta's stability. This mixture of democratic, oligarchic and aristocratic elements is in fact reflected in the *Laws*, though Plato never mentions the term *politeia meikte* (mixed constitution) or *memeigmene* (mixed). What Plato makes use of in the *Laws* is the term *metrios* (moderate) or *metriotes* (moderation), which is equally interesting as it really implies 'moderate' rather than just 'middle' and was his solution for the finding of eurythmia in society:

> A constitution must partake of them both (democracy, monarchy) if there is to be freedom and friendship together with wisdom... now the Persians have cultivated the monarchical element alone, and we the element of freedom, more than is proper; neither of us has preserved the mean between them [*ta metria touton*] but your states, the Lacedaemonian and the Cretan have done so more.[91]

Thus, legislation must attain the mean between despotism and freedom if it is to bring about wisdom, freedom and friendship in the state.

This idea of the middle way, *meden agan* (nothing in excess) was indeed one of the oldest and most widely accepted canons of Greek life and thought, that the good man is to be found in the avoidance of excess, and that to be happy he must respect the limits in his life and be aware that they should not be transgressed in any way. The idea of the 'middle way' was a current tradition

---

[90] Plato, *Laws*, 690.

[91] Ibid., 693d–e. The terms *metrion* (moderate) and *metron* (measure) can be found frequently in the *Laws*, though they had also been used in other Platonic dialogues.

metrion: Plato, *Protagoras*, 338b; *Cratylus*, 414c; *Republic*, v 470d–e; *Theaetetus*, 181b 2 – *Phaedrus*, 229 1–1 *Timeaus*, 65e 2; *Politicus*, 283e 11, 284a 2; *Philebus*, 24c 7, 66a 7; *Laws*, III 690e 4, 4, 6; lc 2, 691d 4,691c 1, 694a 3–1 *Laws*, IV 718a 3, 719c 4,4; *Laws*, V 741c 4; *Laws*, VI 773d 3–1 *Laws*, X c 6–1 *Laws*, XI 918d 1, 920c 3; *Laws*, XII 959d 2.

metron: Plato, *Laws*, III 692a 8, 698b 1; *Laws*, IV 716c 4, 719e 2; *Laws*, V 744e 3; *Laws*, VI 756b 6; *Laws*, VIII 836a 6, 843e 4, 846c 8; *Laws*, XII 944b 2, 959a 3, 957a 4.

in Plato's day and had been ever since Homer and Solon.[92] We are told that when the latter sought advice from the Oracle of Delphi before making his reforms, he sat in the middle of the boat, which he took as an injunction to follow the middle way. Furthermore, when he legislated for Athens, he refused to accept in full the claims of either party but instead attempted to keep both parties content.[93]

Plato himself made use of the terms *metron* (measure) and *meikton* (mixed) quite frequently in his writings, particularly in dialogues which may be perhaps very close in date to the *Laws*. *Philebus* has the good life for man appearing not as pure pleasure, nor even as pure knowledge, but as a mixture of the two, and in the metaphysics of this dialogue Plato offers a mixture of *peras* and *apeiron*. In *Timeaus*, the *kosmios* itself is described as a mixture of necessity and persuasion, and the world soul is a mixture of divisible and indivisible being, sameness and otherness.

In the case of the *Laws*, this idea is first suggested in the structure of the dialogue with the Athenian stranger discoursing upon and correcting the practices of his two Dorian companions who represent Sparta and Crete, and is later found in several aspects of Magnesia. The latter will be mixed like a crater of wine;[94] the legislators will attain the mean between despotism and freedom[95] and will produce the most stable constitution as its form of government will be a mixture of oligarchy and democracy – indeed, the only current forms of government in the cities of the Greek world in the fourth century.[96]

The citizen of Magnesia will be moderate with respect to pleasures,[97] to gains and in his dealing with his fellows, and will make modest offerings to the Gods[98] and ensure proper marriage by encouraging a mixture of families with contrasting qualities.[99] Above all, Magnesia is to be a state of mixed laws and constitution where justice is a mixture of prudence, temperance and courage, whilst its Nocturnal Council is a mixture of the old and young.[100]

---

[92] Plutarch, *Solon*, 14.
[93] Aristotle, *The Athenian Constitution*, XII.
[94] Plato, *Laws*, 773d.
[95] Ibid., 691.
[96] Tyranny was also a well-known form of government in the Greek world but not so common in the fourth century BC.
[97] Plato, *Laws*, 816b.
[98] Ibid., 920d.
[99] Ibid., 631e.
[100] Ibid., 951d.

Aristotle ought to be considered here, both as evidence of the prevalence of these ideas and to claim Plato's influence, as he, too, in his *Nicomachean Ethics*, notes that *arete* is a mean, middle state between opposite extremes reflecting thus the old phrase of *meden agan* (nothing in excess).[101] More importantly, the institutional structure of his *Polity*[102] is a mixture of oligarchic and democratic principles and institutions. However, socially it is not a mixture or balance between rich and poor, but a constitution where the middle class is dominant. This is due to Aristotle's belief that only if the middle class is dominant will stability and justice be reached in the state. For Aristotle, extremes of wealth and poverty are likely to prevent the development of virtue.

Tyranny was also a well known form of government in the Greek world but not so common in the fourth century BC.

To put forward his plan where law will be a master over both the subjects and over the rulers, Plato describes the instruments of government necessary if such a mixed or middle way is to be formulated in a Greek city of his time. He legislates for a popular assembly,[103] admission to which is the privilege of all citizens, and which will have regular meetings fixed by law. Attendance in the assembly is compulsory for all citizens of the first and second property class, with a fine of ten drachmas for absence, but optional for the two lower classes except when the magistrates have called for a full assembly.[104] This proposal seems to give equal power to the people, as even those of the two lower classes are allowed to be present in the decision-making body whilst being paid for their presence. I suspect that the amount of money gained by the participation of the people in the assembly would not be too great and thus the two lower classes would be the ones more attracted to it.

However, though this is evidently a democratic element of Magnesia, it has often received the critical attention of modern philosophers such as Morrow who has felt that the number of people to be elected in the assembly is seemingly odd and inconsistent. However, what is significant is not the details of Plato's account here, but whether he gets his point across well. The principles he adopts and reflects here are worth noting, as they are unlike his previous apprehension and hesitancy as to the validity of popular decisions. This I believe, is the reason why Aristotle, who also devotes critical attention to the election, does not bring up any of the 'difficulties' Morrow picks out.[105]

---

[101] Plato, *Theaetetus*, 152a.
[102] Aristotle, *Politics*.
[103] Plato, *Laws*, 753b, 785b.
[104] Ibid., 764a.
[105] G. Morrow, *Plato's Cretan City*, chapter V, 'government.'

What we ought also to note is the importance Plato places on the magistrates, for, as he tells us, '...nothing so far as possible is to be left without a guard' and he includes in this scheme the thirty-seven *nomophylakes, the agoranomoi*, the *agronomoi*, and three generals. This is a clear indication of Plato's close acquaintance with the judicial system of Athens, a system where most legal issues were settled on court and where the magistrates played a very substantial role in the administration of justice. Thus, in Magnesia, the judicial functions are performed both by the *archai* and by the *dikasteria* and, indeed, the two are interrelated and complementary institutions since it is the magistrates who first hear the charges and then bring them into court in order to be judged by the *dikasts*.

Of the magistrates, the *nomophylakes*, the major guardians of the laws, are by far the most important officials in Plato's constitution, as they have the responsibility of supervising the other magistrates. The *agoranomoi*, who are situated around the *agora*, protect and defend the city against the enemy, whereas the *agronomoi*, his third set of officers, are entrusted with the task of policing and protecting the country outside the city. Aristotle tells us that officials of this sort with responsibility for looking after the *chora* and ta *exo tou asteos* are called by some agronomoi and by others *yloroi*.[106]

Nevertheless, we have no evidence that a set of *agronomoi* existed in Athens, but whether they existed or not and in which Greek city or cities is not what matters here. What is of vital importance is Plato's emphasis on the duty of the magistrates to carry the right to punish for violations of the law and for breaches of public order in the various areas under their control, and his notion that every magistrate must also be a judge in some matters.[107] Plato allows the magistrates to express judicial powers sometimes, as in the case of citizens' failure to vote or to get married, or their careless use of fire or their contribution to damage of public buildings.[108]

What is equally striking is Plato's imposition of penalties upon the magistrates to the effect that if any magistrate appears to have shown injustice in imposing penalties he shall be liable for double the amount to the injured party. Moreover, an unjust decision by a magistrate with respect to any claim may be brought before the public courts by anyone who wishes to do so.[109] Plato tells us that if the *agronomoi* commit any act of insolence in the matters

---

[106] Aristotle, *Politics*, 1232b 28–30.
[107] Plato, *Republic* 767a.
[108] Plato, *Laws*, 765d (failure to vote); 774d (failure to get married); 764, 779 (damage of public building); 843e (careless use of fire).
[109] Ibid., 846b.

over which they have supervision, injured parties may bring a suit in the common courts and if successful will receive double damages.[110]

The right of citizens to bring a suit was a standard Athenian procedure in the fifth and fourth centuries, as is clear from the orators. Aristotle once again tells us that in the Draconian reforms Draco had provided that anyone who thought he had been wronged by a magistrate could lay his grievance before the Areopagus, and that Solon had also provided for appeal to the courts.[111]

Another point which is worth stressing here is Plato's treatment of the issue of collective and individual responsibility.[112] Clearly, the magistrates exercised their judicial functions as a group and not individually. This was also a principle embedded in Athenian practice. From the time of Solon, at least, all Athenian magistrates acted as committees and the development of collectivism in Attica was closely connected with the development of democracy. It definitely brought more citizens into official positions whilst it prevented the rise of any hierarchy within the board of magistrates, emphasising the fundamental equality of its members. At the same time, it provided a measure of protection against arbitrary or malicious administration, a protection obviously necessary after these offices began to be filled by lot. Nowhere else, so far as we know, was the principle of collectivism so generally followed.

It is after Plato has legislated for the magistrates that the interlocutors became jurists with the task of finding how justice is distributed and exercised Plato's emphasis on jurisprudence become more evident. It is his notion of jurisprudence that helped him to find the way to give each person his due and a harmonious arrangement in life, or what Aristotle called *Táxis* (order).

What is noticeable here is that Plato's whole account of the courts justifies his will to distribute more power to the individual and yet make him depend on the state and look to the latter for support as he still understands that it is difficult for the multitude to judge well:

> A *dikast* who is without voice and who does not have more to say in the examination than the contending parties... would not be adequate to decide questions of justice; therefore it is not easy for a multitude to judge well nor for a small court either if its members are ordinary [ ].[113]

---

[110] Plato, *Laws*, 761–762b.
[111] Aristotle, *The Athenian Constitution*, L III, 6.
[112] Plato, *Laws,* 76ld–c, 764b–c, 834d–e, 844L–d, 845c, 846a, 847a–b, 879e.
[113] Ibid., 766d.

Plato understands the necessity for popular participation in the administration of justice through courts, although '...in a city where the *dikasteries* (i.e. the *dikasts*) are ordinary and without voice and conceal the opinions and decide a case severely or what is even more dangerous when they are not silent but full of tumult – like theatres applauding and hooting in turn this or that orator – then there is a very serious evil that affects the whole state'.[114]

Whether the state Plato has in mind here is Athens or not, we cannot tell. What we can deduce is that most of the judicial characteristics Plato attributes to Magnesia can be found in the Athenian society of his time. In spite of the fact that Plato is always aware of the failings of public judgement, though not as much as at the time of the *Republic*, he now expresses a characteristic dogma of his time, as he understands that, 'He who is without the right of sitting with his fellows in the courts of law thinks that he is without a share in the city.'[115] This sentiment well expressed in Aristotle's *Politics* where a citizen is defined as somebody who participates in the deliberation and administration of justice.[116] Yet Plato tells us that '...in a state where the courts have the best possible constitution, those who are to be judges will be well trained and tested'.[117] I take this statement to be in complete harmony with the one expressed before, in the sense that Plato is referring to different courts: the popular court where he expresses a democratic principle due to its popular participation, and a higher court with well-tested judges which rules over the popular court and limits its power.

The lower ranks of society are now given some political rights and powers, though careful regulations always ensure that they will not attain political control. It is at this point that Plato's distinction of *idia* and *demosia*,[118] private and public or common courts, is explained in detail though not actually in principle. It is a distinction that is based on his idea that 'A Society as we know, will soon become no society at all without only appointed courts of justice'.[119]

Plato distinguishes between two kinds of courts, the private courts which are concerned with private litigation and which in return are subdivided into three categories, and the public courts which function 'when a citizen thinks

---

[114] Plato, *Laws*, 876d.
[115] Ibid., 768b.
[116] Aristotle, *Politics*, 1275a 22–23.
[117] Plato, *Laws*, 876c.
[118] Ibid., 767b 5–9.
[119] Ibid., 766d.

that someone is injuring *(adikei)* the state *(demosion)* and wishes to come to the community's assistance *"tó koino"* (public).'[120]

At this point, I must note that though I am aware of the apparent inconsistencies contained in Plato's detailed account of the courts, these do not concern me here, partly because they have been investigated by others and partly because I view the principles, that of popular participation in particular, contained in Plato's account, as far more important than the inconsistencies of its details. Thus, the *Laws* gives a clearer answer than before to the argument of Callicles in *Gorgias*,[121] and to that of Glaucon in the *Republic*[122] in that it does more than just state that justice is not conventional and is not simply what is advantageous for the stranger, as Thrasymachus, who is caricatured in *Republic* Book I, is said to have argued. Indeed, in the *Republic Plato* provides his answer as to what justice is, viewing the latter as a psychic and social harmony, but the task of developing this in detail is left to the *Laws*, where justice depends on laws and it is laws that limit the powers of those who are given the right to apply and distribute it.

What is also striking is Plato's understanding of the corruptibility of human nature, and his consequent intention to ensure that the members of any court do not act according to their personal criteria and sympathies but always give the right judgement.[123] Every judge is individually responsible for his actions and for his decisions, as already explained. Similarly, any Magnesian will be punished if it is found that he has committed a voluntary act of injustice, as Plato now understands that there can be such acts, though in a very limited sense, that is, to the extent that the criminal lacks moral knowledge or that the crime took place due to an accident or to a similar cause.

Here, for the last time, Plato recasts his views on voluntary and involuntary crimes. However, the foundations of Plato's moral views as developed in the *Laws* could be found in early and middle period dialogues – *Protagoras, Meno, Gorgias* and *the Republic* – where Plato had been concerned with finding a way to remove the criminal's evil disposition as that was to the disadvantage of the latter and therefore against his true desires and best interests. Thus, Plato arrives at a paradox in the sense that the criminal is an involuntary criminal, and should not be blamed but helped to cure himself, willingly and voluntarily accepting his own punishment.

---

[120] Plato, *Laws*, 767b 5–9.
[121] Plato, *Gorgias*, 483.
[122] Plato, *Republic*, 358–359.
[123] Plato, *Laws*, 767e.

In order to lead the criminal to the understanding that virtue is happiness, and vice is a disease, Plato equates the role of the legislators–jurists with that of educators as it is also their task to educate man to avoid the disorder of the baser parts of their souls, that is, to improve the subjects of Magnesia.

Plato makes use of this medical metaphor familiar from *Gorgias*[124] and also found in the *Republic*,[125] where punishment is metaphorically described as therapy, and in the *Sophist*[126] where punishment as education is described as analogous to medical therapy. In the *Laws*,[127] the good doctor, Plato tells us, is something of a philosopher, since both men use medicine in order to cure the patient of his disease. The good doctor is he who has a good understanding of the patient's physiology and having diagnosed the cause of the illness prescribes the medicine required for his efficient cure. The philosopher–legislator, before offering his penology, also needs to understand carefully the psychic and mental state of the patient, thus finding the roots of his disease through his discussion with the patient about the source of illness and about physiology in general.

Plato notes that the criminal must be made a better man,[128] a man who will understand for himself why he ought to embrace justice, hate injustice and willingly seek his punishment, an idea Plato held throughout his entire career.

In *Protagoras*, a dialogue concerned with the demonstration of the superficiality of the Sophists' ethical and political views, Plato notes that '...if a man knows what is good and what is bad nothing will induce him to do other than as reason bids (i.e. pursue the good), for knowledge is enough support for man'.[129] But '...a man may recognise the best and be able to do it, but yet he may refrain, and do something else because he is overcome by pleasure, anger, fear or other emotions'.[130] Plato concludes that '...being overcome by pleasure'[131] should properly be ascribed to ignorance, so that if a man fails it is because he is ignorant. His ignorance implies his failure, and his failure in turn implies his unwilling wrongness. Thus, what man needs is knowledge which will alone be sufficient and necessary for virtue, an idea that goes back to Socrates. However, Plato attempts to show the unsoundness of Protagoras'

---

[124] Plato, *Gorgias*, 487a.
[125] Plato, *Republic*, 409a, 445a.
[126] Plato, *Sophist*, 224a.
[127] Plato, *Laws*, 857a–b, 859c–e.
[128] Ibid., 862.
[129] Plato, *Protagoras*, 352c.
[130] Ibid., 352d.
[131] Ibid., 357d.

view in the sense that virtue cannot be taught. The Protagorean view is flawed, since its supporter thinks of virtue as a collection of qualities, failing to see that virtue and knowledge are synonymous, and thus he does not actually know what virtue is. Nevertheless, both Protagoras and Socrates share a common view in this dialogue, which is that rational punishment should be set not in terms of what has happened, that is the past, but with what must happen, in order to prevent the offender from committing the same act in the future. Punishment is seen as a way of reforming criminals and of leading them to the state of virtue. It implies the education of criminals and the retaliation for their offence, an idea that Plato apparently attacks here, though comes to accept in subsequent dialogues.

Similarly, in *Gorgias* Plato holds that doing wrong is worse than suffering it, and that wrongdoers who escape punishment suffer more than those who receive punishment. He attacks Polus' reiteration of Gorgias' claim[132] that the powerful are those with political influence, such as orators and tyrants, making Socrates claim that such men do not do what they really want but what appears to them to be the best. Thus, Plato, having allowed Polus to express the conventional view of prudence and to associate knowledge with power and ignorance with weakness, makes him see the wrongness of his position in the sense that the criminal's actions are not actually his own choosing but are a result of his ignorance.

While for Callicles the powerful and thus happy man is he who uses force to rule over the weak, for Socrates the powerful man is happy only when his happiness consists in his virtue and not in his taking advantage of the distribution of goods. Yet he understands that a man like Archelaus should not be held responsible for his wrong actions as 'no one errs willingly'.[133] In the *Republic*, Plato explicitly adopts Protagoras' own penal theory, since he demonstrates that virtue is taught whilst admitting the possibility of *akrasia*, that is, man's moral failure. The situation envisaged in the *Republic* may be illustrated by the following example. A man led by his appetites may desire to swim after having

---

[132] Plato, *Gorgias*, 466e ff.

[133] It is useful, I feel, to parallel the ideas of Socrates and Plato with that of St. Paul who claims that no one errs willingly: 'we want some things but we do others'. Romans 7, 19–23. According to St. Paul, the evil is rooted in our own nature. Our understanding knows what is good but we do what we don't actually wish – the evil. The cause of this is to be found in something 'dark' and metaphysical that we have inherited with our body thus, the evil is inside us from birth – in contrast to Socrates who thinks that we can escape from doing Nvrong when we receive the proper education. In other words, Socrates believes in the human capacity to overcome evil in contrast to St. Paul who expects this help to come from the goodness of God.
See also Aristotle, *Nicomachean Ethics*, 1179 b 2–10.

his meal, but he is prevented from doing so by his reason which warns him that this might lead to his death. The fact that he does not swim is attributed to his reason's powerful rule and control over his desires. But if his reason did not compel him, the man would swim and possibly die.

Thus it is reason that makes the decisions, the spirited element involving courage that makes certain that the orders of reason are carried out, so that reason rules desire. Justice turns out to be the health and harmony of the soul whereas injustice its disease and discord. It is the cure of injustice that receives Plato's attention once again as he attempts to find a way to heal the patient and help him get rid of his moral disease, provided the criminal is curable.

In order to make the criminal more *sophron* (self-controlled), Plato notes that *sophrosyne* is a matter of education which in return helps the criminal to understand the function of punishment. But what is also striking here is Plato's suggestion that we ought to discriminate between the curable and the incurable criminal and treat each differently in the same way that different social classes should be treated differently; equal people equally and unequal people unequally. Plato appreciates here that those who benefit from punishment are those who have committed curable crimes.[134] They benefit in two ways, both to the effect that they will get rid of the evil and that they will be equally beneficial to their fellow citizens as they will serve as an example to all those who are frightened by the prospect of being punished and so will eventually aim at improving themselves also. This idea brings in an element of deterrence otherwise not strongly present in Plato's humanitarian – medical theory of punishment, yet he understands that there could be criminals who have committed incurable crimes and are thus no longer susceptible to benefit. In *Timeaus*[135] Socrates argues that no one desires evil and that, no one is voluntarily evil, as evil is a matter of physical weakness or disease and bad upbringing. However, as all three are beyond our control, evil can occur, but no one should be blamed as it occurs regardless of our will. So we should attribute the cause of our disease to our political and educational background as well as to our parents who have brought us up.[136]

In the *Laws*, Plato, recasting his previous views, implements a very extensive moral psychology. He takes a particular interest in the suffering of the victim, with an equally detailed theory of punishment which responds to a great number of questions. The reader may be concerned with the amount of

---

[134] Plato, *Gorgias*, 487a 7.
[135] Plato, *Timeaus*, 86b ff.
[136] Ibid., 86b; Plato, *Republic*, 444b 8 ff.

reform needed by the criminal and offered to him in return by the state. In attempting to find an answer to the above questions, he may also notice that Plato's overoptimistic view of human nature as expressed in the *Republic* is now replaced by a rather pessimistic view which is nevertheless more close to true life – how life is actually lived by real people. This is based on the idea that although the soul is the most divine of all of man's possessions, man can indeed fail to honour his soul both voluntarily and involuntarily. Indeed, in Book V, Plato states the Socratic paradox that 'no one does wrong willingly' or 'no one is willingly bad'.[137] I believe that Book V serves as an introduction to the fully detailed discussion that follows in Book IX where the Athenian, being aware that crime does exist, proposes analogous measures according to the causes of crime and to every criminal, reinforcing both his medical analogy and the idea that death is preferable to continue life with a diseased soul. In short, in Book IX, Plato plays down the paradox that 'no one does wrong willingly', understanding the difficulty it causes, as he appreciates that some acts may be called voluntary whereas others are involuntary, regardless of either the benefit or injury they bring. He understands that injuries may be sustained either by accident or by deliberation, so that there exist voluntary crimes. The latter take place due to the criminal's lack of moral knowledge or because of accident or some other similar cause. This line of thought is due to Plato's appreciation that if no crimes were voluntary then there should be no punishment.

As elsewhere in his works, Plato thinks the criminal must be taught, as he believes that man is naturally good and that no man will choose to be a criminal if he realises where his true interests lie; there is no need to relate the interests of the criminal to any rights he may have, as Plato does not think in terms of rights. What he does think is that legislators need to be jurists in that they need to analyse the basis of every crime and treat the criminal accordingly, but on the whole they must attack and outlaw retribution. They must enforce capital punishment when the criminal is incurable but pre-empt execution for the curable. Criminals who are found incurable must be removed from the state, as otherwise they will harm the curable. Plato does not allow even for the possibility of expelling them from the state, because if they have committed wretched acts they may commit other such acts when transferred to another state, due to their incurability. This attitude is different from punishment to deter the rest, as it is advocated to protect others. In short, Plato implicitly allows the remission to the state of bad citizens that

---

[137] Plato, *Laws*, 728c–735e.

might be curable,[138] offering them every opportunity to participate in the organisation of the state once they agree to reform themselves and be educated in a way in which they will *acquire phronesis*.

In order to help them acquire this, Plato thinks that a judicial system with courts as its instruments is necessary, where laws enforced by the legislators and carried out by the jurists will help the citizens to teach themselves and cure the disease of their souls.

The criminal is pitied, and if found curable is given the opportunity to cure himself, whereas if found incurable he will be executed in order to remove his own evil psychic state and evil influence on his fellows. At this point, one could argue against Plato in that he was in a way enforcing fears of impiety. Should people be executed because they were ignorant in honouring the Gods?

In this sense, it could be said that Plato's position is like that of a utilitarian, as a small number of people would be punished in the interests of the many. However, his view is not like the strictly utilitarian one, in that his notion of punishment is different from punishment to deter, since the reason for executing the incurables is for the sake of the safety of others. Yet the reader needs to note here that utilitarian is an anachronism in a discussion of Plato.

Yet, Plato is certainly preaching here for humanitarian treatment of the curable criminal who, with the help of the legislator, will be made a better man, both in his character as well as in his conduct of his affairs in Magnesia. The legislator should not obtain consent by violence but by persuasion:[139] hence the use of the preambles that would set out the motives for obeying the *Laws*.[140]

In other words, what is recommended for the last time by Plato is that *timoria* (punishment, revenge) should be seen as a *therapeia* (therapy, cure)[141] that is characterised by a notion *epieikeia* (fairness) and will repair the damage caused by the victim, whilst curing the offender's vicious soul and thus his psychic disease.

In short, Plato is still arguing against men who give free rein to their passions. He is opposed to the Sophists and the tragedians who considered the Gods as human inventions[142] and so led to the relativity and instability of

---

[138] Plato, *Laws*, 736c 2.
[139] Ibid., 8887a ff.
[140] Ibid., 719c–723b.
[141] Ibid., 862. See also Mackenzie, 1981.
[142] Ibid., 891b–899d.

human affairs; they led men to doubt that divine justice enters into the details of human affairs.[143] Hence Plato's last attempt to offer 'a true tragedy', a pattern upon which education should be based.

---

[143] Plato, *Laws*, 899d–905.

Epilogue

'Many people, few ideas: we all think more or less the same, and we exchange, borrow, steal thoughts from one another.'

Milan Kundera
Immortality

My analysis of the *Laws* has shown that the dialogue is not just a treatise for the construction and organisation of a new state, or a religious poem, or a treatise on jurisprudence. All the above descriptions are *aspects* of its drama, bus no one of them on its own reflects accurately the full import of the work. A part is not equivalent to the whole. Although I accept all the above descriptions since the *Laws* does describe a new state, it expresses Plato's religious beliefs; and contains a section on *dikonomia* or jurisprudence (in the modem meaning of the word in English), it is erroneous, I believe, when a single part or aspect of the dialogue is been taken to characterise the whole. In this way, each of the above descriptions, although not entirely wrong, nevertheless ignores the actual intention, substance and meaning of the dialogue Plato intended to get across to his audience. Furthermore, it partly destroys the essence of the work, because it is concerned not with what Plato must have intended to say but with the intentions, sympathies and preoccupations of the author of the description. The assumption that the *Laws* is a work on 'jurisprudence', for example, may allow some of those who take the work in their hands to believe that this was indeed Plato's aim, and thus misconceive the actual meaning of the work.

There is no doubt that the approach to the *Laws* I have followed disturbs many modern interpretative assumptions. However, I have tried as hard as I could to do justice to the *Laws*, and Plato's description of the work as his 'truest tragedy' in particular, by meeting its challenge in my description of the *Laws* as drama.

I believe all the above descriptions made by knowledgeable scholars as simply subordinate to its drama: they are the teachings which emerge from its dramatic meaning. They are simple teachings describing an everyday reality, and so are intended to suit an average citizen, just as the institution of tragedy was also suited to an average citizen and aimed to educate him. But this Platonic, tragedy although comparable to those of the dramatists, is of a different kind, a kind that has proper *paideia* in its heart, intending to teach the individual the way to use his reason properly. It could be said to signify the age of reason.

Yet the *Laws* aims to influence and challenge the way the Greeks understand the relation between drama and philosophy. If tragedy is to fulfil its goals, it will have to be placed within the philosophical context of reasoning and must, describe the best and most noble life. Indeed, the *Laws* could provide the right model for the education of the citizens of Magnesia, in contrast to Greek tragedies that on the whole gave the wrong models of life to people, being were more concerned with their own effects than with anything that actually mattered. This is in contrast to the *Laws*, which represents what is truly serious – that is, how the fine and noble life could be acquired by the citizens of the new state.

Although *nomoi* means laws, it is more than Plato's giving of laws to suit his new state. This misunderstanding that the *Laws* is a mere code of laws is due to the fact that we have translated the title *Nomoi* as 'Laws', considering the *Laws* of Plato to have the same implications as what we now understand by the term law and how the latter is used in modern legal theory. *Nomos* in ancient Greece meant both convention as well as written law.

For Plato, *nomos* is an instrument or a tool, a means for the achievement of his goals, an end in itself, as his laws embody a certain vision of the world, a vision of the right and the good which would be appropriate to implement in the society of Magnesia; above all, his laws have *paideutic* meaning so that they are the Magnesian's teachers and parents. Hence Plato's urge that the legislators must prepare the citizens to accept the laws through artful preambles; he likens the good legislator to the freeman's doctor, who does not proceed to the administration of a therapy before he has thoroughly discussed the matter with and convinced his patient.

The *Laws* is a 'true tragedy', indeed a philosophical–religious drama, a kind of drama which contains its own critical principles, and in which Plato masterfully and harmoniously combines his political, philosophical and religious insights with his capacity to write as a philosophical dramatist.

Plato gives his audience the means necessary to acquire virtue: the fine and noble life. Politics, ethics and jurisprudence do contribute to the accomplishment of his tragedy, but they are the parts of the whole, that is, they are the components of its drama.

To some critics, this conclusion may seem rambling; to me it seems right, as I conceive every argument and fact given in the *Laws* to serve its purpose, that is, to help Plato emphasise the ramifications of human life, from birth to death. To achieve his task he has had to be a dramatist, a lawgiver, an educator, a penologist, a juror, a judge and, above all, a true philosopher with a clean soul, as only by combining all the above virtues is he able to satisfy his required sense of tragedy and educate the new citizens politically, socially, morally and legally. Moreover, his combination of all the above virtues enables him to show the dramatists that instead of being concerned mainly with the techniques of their works, as they apparently had nothing new to say, they should be concerned with and pay their attention to serious existing problems.

Indeed, the *Laws*, although not the most artfully written tragedy in the technical sense, is concerned with something that matters, and shows that the spirit and method of tragedy should be of a different kind from that which was current in ancient Athens. The stage technique of tragedy does not matter for Plato; he would possibly prefer his audience to read the *Laws* as he understands that it could not really be performed in theatre. This is the reason why he wishes this discussion to become a text in the education of the Magnesians.

In concluding, I may say that at a time when people wander amidst glorious ruins without memory, pray without faith, bathe in the light without vision, and have philosophy, religion and art in their pockets, there is also the frightening possibility that works of great importance, like those of Plato and the *Laws* in particular, will be and are in fact misinterpreted. This is because supposedly good, sensitive and knowledgeable scholars when writing on Plato, miss points of primary and vital importance in their academic works in order to enable themselves to build doctrines which they will then attribute to Plato. In this way, they perform the part which the Sophists and dramatists performed in the fifth and fourth centuries in ancient Greece, rather than that of true and genuine philosophers. So, although in our times there are many kinds of philosophy, the real philosophy is absent because our thoughts have been subjected to our time.

This was indeed the reason that impelled me to study the *Laws*, as I felt that Plato's own criticism of his work as the *'truest tragedy'* has received little or no consideration at all in modern scholarship. My hope has now been fulfilled, whatever its merit is. I hope to have been constructive in my research, although I do not claim to have found indisputable ways of looking at the *Laws*. As things stand, I have ended up with a book whose parts could be read independently and yet which forms a whole, so that the reader who will go through the entire manuscript might not be without rewards, as originality often consists not only in having new thoughts, but in making clear what was not clear before.

Bibliography

General

The following list contains full details of all the books and articles referred to or mentioned in the text or notes. In addition, I have included works which although I have had no occasion to mention in the course of my book, they have been of great interest to me, and particularly useful in my understanding of the *Laws*.

Acton, H.B., *The Philosophy of Punishment*, London, 1969
Adkins, A.W.H., 'Homeric Values and Homeric Society', *JHS*, (1971), pp.1–14
Adkins, A.W.H., 'Honour and Punishment in the Homeric Epics', *BICS*, (1960), pp.7, 23–32
Anderson, O., 'Some Thought on the Shield of Achilles in Symbolae Osloenses', 51 (1976), pp.5–18
Andrewes, A., *Greek Society*, London, 1986
Annas, J., *An Introduction to Plato's Republic*, Oxford, 1981
Annas, J., 'Plato's Myths of Judgement', *Phronesis*, pp.27, 119–143
Arieti, J.A., *Interpreting Plato – the Dialogues as Drama*, Maryland, 1991
Athanasakis, A., *The Orphic Hymns*, Text and Translation, Scholars Press, USA, 1988

Barker, E., *Greek Political Theory – Plato and his Predecessors*, London–New York, 1979, pp.342–345
Barker, E., *The Political Thought of Plato and Aristotle*, New York, 1959
Barker, E., *Greek Political Thoughts* 1960
Baldry, H.C., *Ancient Culture and Society – The Greek Tragic Theatre*, London, 1978
Bennett, E.L., *The Pylos Tablets. A Preliminary Transcription*, Princeton, 1951
Bennett, E.L., *The Pylos Tablets. Texts of the Inscriptions Found 1939–1954*, University of Cincinnati, 1955
Bernardete, S., 'Hesiod's *Works and Days*: a first reading, in *Agon*, 1967, 1

Biscardi, A., *Diritto Greco Antico*, Milano, 1982
Bloom, A., *The Republic of Plato*, New York, 1968
Bluestone, H.N., *Women and the Ideal Society*, Oxford, 1987
Boeckh, A., *Commentaria in Platonia qui vulgo Fertum Minoem*, Halle, 1806
Bowra, C.M., *The Greek Experience*, Oxford, 1973
Bowra, C.M., *Sophoclean Tragedy*, Oxford, 1944
Bowra, C.M., *Tradition and Design in the Iliad*, Oxford, 1968
Brown, W., 'Land Tenure in Mycenaean Pylos', *Historia*, vol. 5 (1956)

Campbell, *The Sophist and Statesman of Plato*, Oxford, 1867
Ciaceri, E., *Storia Della Magna Grecia*, Milano, 1928
Cornford, F.M., *Plato's Theory of Knowledge*, London, 1935
Cross, R.C. and Woozley, A.D., *Plato's Republic: a Philosophical Commentary*, London, 1964
Crossey, J., *Ancients and Moderns: Essays on the Tradition of Political Philosophy in Honor of Leo Strauss*, New York, 1964

Dodds, E.R., *The Greeks and the Irrational*, London, 1951
Dodds, E.R., 'Homer and the Analysis', Oxford, (1968), pp.1–17
Dodds, E.R., 'Notes on *The Oresteia*', *CQ*, (1953), pp. 11–21
Dodds, E.R., 'Plato and the Irrational', *JHS*, (1945), pp.16–25
Dodds, E.R., *Plato: Gorgias*, Oxford, 1959
Dover, K.J., *Aristophanic Comedy*, 1972
Dover, K.J., *Greek Homosexuality*, London, 1978
Dover, K.J., 'Some Neglected Aspects of Agamemnon's Dilemma', *JHS*, (1973), pp. 58–69
Dover, K.J. et al., *Ancient Greek Literature*, Oxford, 1980

England, E.B., *The Laws of Plato*, Manchester, 1921
Evans, A., 'The Palace of Minos at Knossos', IV, London (I 924–1936)
Evans, J., 'Excavations in the Neolithic Settlement of Knossos', *BSA*, 59 (1964), pp. 132–240

Fiebleman, J.K., *Religious Platonism – the Influence of Religion on Plato and the Influence of Plato on Religion*, London, 1959
Finley, M.I., *The Ancient Greeks*, London, 1963
Finley, M.I., 'Homer and Mycenae Property and Tenure', *Historia*, 6 (1984)
Finley, M.I., *Politics in the Ancient World*, Oxford, 1984

Finley, M.I. 'The Problem of the Unity of Greek Law', *ACI*, 5D Firenze (1966), pp.129–142
Finley M.I., *The World of Odysseus*, London, 1964
Friedlander, P., *Plato: An Introduction*, Princeton, 1969

Gagarin, M., 'Dikê in the *Works and Days*', *CPl, (*1973)
Gagarin, M., 'Dikê in Archaic Greek Thought', *CPl, (*1974)
Gagarin, M., *Early Greek Law*, London, 1968
Gagarin, M., 'Hesiod's Dispute with Perses' in *Transactions of the APA*, 104 (1974)
Glotz, G., *La Solidarité dans le droit criminel en Grèce*, Paris, 1904
Glotz, G., *La Cité Grecque*, trans. in Greek by Agnes Sakellariou, 3rd edn., Athens, 1989
Gomme, A.W., 'The Position of Women in Athens in the Fifth and Fourth Centuries BC', *CPh*, 20 (1925), 1–25
Gould, J., *The Development of Plato's Ethics*, Cambridge, 1955.
Gouldner, A.W., *Enter Plato: Classical Greece and the Origins of Social Theory*, New York, 1965
Guthrie, W.K.C., *A History of Greek Philosophy*
Guthrie, W.K.C., 'Early Greek Religion in the Light of the Decipherment of Linear B', *Inst Cl*, 6 (1959), pp. 35–46
Guthrie, W.K.C., *The Greeks and their Gods*, Boston, 1955
Guthrie, W.K.C. 'Plato's Views on the Nature of Soul' in G. Vlastos, *Plato*, II, pp.230–243
Guthrie, W.K.C. *The Sophists*, Cambridge, 1971

Habermas, J., *Knowledge and Human Interests*, trans., Shapiro, J.J., Boston, Beacon, 1971 (1968)
Halliwell, S., *Plato: Republic* V, Warminster, 1993
Harrison, J., *Epilegomena to the Study of Greek Religion*, Cambridge, 1921
Harrison, J., *Prolegomena to the Study of Greek Religion*, chapters 9–12, New York, 1922
Harrison, J., *Themis, a Study of the Social Origins of Greek Religion*, London, 1963
Havelock, E.A., *The Greek Concept of Justice*, Cambridge, Mass., 1978
Havelock, E.A., *The Greek Concept of Justice*, Harvard, 1978
Havelock, E.A., *The Greek Concept of Justice from its Shadow in Homer to its Substance in Plato*, Harvard, 1978
Havelock, E.A., *Preface to Plato*, Harvard, 1963
Hegel, G.W.F., *Lectures on the Philosophy of World History*

Heidel, W., *Pseudo-Platonica*, Baltimore, 1896
Humphreys, S.C., *The Anthropology of the Greeks*, London, 1915
Hyland, D., *Why Plato Wrote Dialogues, Philosophy and Rhetoric*, 1968

Jaeger, W., *Paideia*, vol. II, London, 1943
Jaeger, W., *Scripta Minora 2*, Rome, 1960

Kahn, C. 'Anaximander's Fragment: The Universe Governed by Law' in Mourelatos (ed.), *The Presocratics*, pp. 99–117
Kant, I., *Critique of Pure Reason*, trans. Norman Kemp Smith, London, 1929
Kirk, G.S., Raven J.E., and Schofield, M., *The Presocratic Scholars*, Cambridge, 1983
Kitto, H.D.F., *Form and Meaning in Drama – a Study of Six Greek Plays and of Hamlet*, New York, 1959
Kitto, H.D.F., *Greek Tragedy – a Literary Study*, London, 1939
Kitto, H.D.F., *The Greeks*, London, 1951
Kitto, H.D.F., *Sophocles, Dramatist and Philosopher*, London, 1958
Kraut, R., *The Cambridge Companion to Plato*, Cambridge, 1992
Kern, O., *Orphicorum Fragmenta*, Berlin, 1921
Klein, J., *'About the Philebus' Interpretation*, vol. 2, no. 3
Klein, J., *A Commentary on Plato's Meno*, North Carolina, 1965

Lacey, W.K., *The Family in Classical Greece*, New York, 1968
Lefkowitz, R. Marg., 'Critical Stereotypes and the Poetry of Sappho', *GRBS*, xiv (1973)
Lesky, Albin, *History of Ancient Greek Literature*, trans. in modern Greek, Thessaloniki, 1972

Mackenzie, M.M., *Plato on Punishment*, Berkeley, Los Angeles and London, 1981
Mackenzie, M.M., 'The Tears of Chryses. Retaliation in the *Iliad*', *Philosophy and Literature*, (1978)
Marinatos, S., 'The Cult of the Cretan Coves' in *Review of Religions* 5, 1940–1
Marinatos, S., in *Bulletin de Correspondence Hellenigne 96*, 1972
Mill, J.S., *On Liberty*, ed. with an introduction by Gertrude Himmelfarb, Penguin Classics, 1987
Montesquieu, *L'Esprit des lois (The Spirit of the Laws)*, trans. T. Nugent, New York, 1949
Morrow, G., 'Plato and the Rule of Law' in G. Vlastos, *Plato*, II, pp. 144–165

Morrow, G., *Plato's Cretan City – a Historical Interpretation of the Laws*, Princeton, 1960
Müller, G., *Shidien zu den platonischen Nomoi*, Munich, 1951, revised edn 1968
Murdoch, Iris, *The Fire and the Sun – Why Plato Banished the Artists*, Oxford, 1977
Murray, G.G.A., *Aeschylus, the Creator of Tragedy*, Oxford, 1940
Murray, G.G.A., *Euripides and his Age*, London, 1946
Murray, G.G.A., *Five Stages of Greek Religion*, Oxford, 1923
Mylonas, G.E., *Ancient Mycenae: the Capital City of Agamemnon*, Princeton, 1961
Mylonas, G.E., 'Homeric and Mycenaean Burial Customs', *JAA*, (1966)
Mylonas, G.E., *Mycenae and the Mycenaean Age*, Princeton, 1966

Nilsson, M.P., *Cults, Myths, Oracles and Politics in Ancient Greece*, Lund, 1951
Nilsson, M.P., *A History of Greek Religion*, Oxford, 1949, pp.225–234
Nilsson, M.P., *The Minoan-Mycenaean Religion and its Survival in Greek Religion*, Lund, 1950
Nilsson, M.P., *The Mycenaean Origin of Greek Mythology*, Berkeley, 1932

Ostwald, M., *Nomos and the Beginning of Athenian Democracy*, Oxford, 1969

Pangle, T., *The Laws of Plato*, New York, Basic Books, 1980
Pangle, T., [ed.] *The Roots of Political Philosophy*
Pavlu, J., *Die Psudoplatonischen Zwillings – dialogue Minos und Hipparch*, Vienna, 1910
Patzer, A., *Die Entstehung der wissenschaftlichen politik bei den Griechen sitz Ber wiss Ges*, Frankfurt, 1966
Planinc, Z., *Plato's Political Philosophy – Prudence in the Republic and the Laws*, London, 1991
Pomeroy, S.B., *Goddesses, Whores, Wives and Slaves – Women in Classical Antiquity*, New York, 1975
Pomeroy, S.B., *Women's History and Ancient History*, North Carolina, 1991
Popper, K., *The Open Society and its Enemies*, vol. 1: *Plato*, London, 1966
Post, L.A., *The Vatican Plato and its Relations*, Middletown, CT, USA, American Philological Association, 1934
Powell, A., *Athens and Sparta: Constructing Greek Political Social History from 476 BC*, London, Routledge, 1985

Rawls, J., *A Theory of Justice*, Oxford, 1986
Reeve, C.D.C., *Philosopher–Kings: the Argument of Plato's Republic*, Princeton, New Jersey, 1988
De Romilly, J., *Problèmes de la démocratic grecque*, Paris, 1975 (trans. in modern Greek by Nikos Agavanakis, Athens, 1992)
Rosen, S., *Plato's Symposium*, Yale, 1968
Rostovtzeff, *A History of the Ancient World*, Oxford, 1929
Rousseau, J.J., *The Social Contract*, trans. and introduced by Maurice Cranston, London, Penguin, 1968
Rowe, C.J., *Plato*, Brighton, 1984
Ryle, G., *Plato's Progress*, Cambridge, 1966

Saunders, T.J., *Bibliography on Plato's Laws: 1920–1976*, 2nd edn., with additional citations to March 1979, New York, 1979
Saunders, T.J., 'Notes on the *Laws* of Plato', *BICS*, Supplement 28 (1972)
Saunders, T.J., *Plato, the Laws*, London, Penguin translation, 1970
Saunders, T.J., *Plato's Penal Code: Tradition, Controversy and Reform in Greek Penology*, Oxford, 1991
Schleiermacher, F., *Uber den wert des Socrates als Philosophen*, Berlin, 1815
Saunders, T.J., 'Two Points in Plato's Penal Code', *CQ*, (1963), pp. 194–199
Sealey, R., *Women and Law in Classical Greece*, North Carolina, 1990
Shorey, P., *Plato's Republic*, Cambridge, 1946
Sinclair, R.K., *Democracy and Participation in Athens*, Cambridge, 1988
Stalley, R.F., *An Introduction to Plato's Laws*, Oxford, 1983
Strauss, L., *What Is Political Philosophy?*, Westport, Greenwood, 1973
Strauss, L., *The City and Man*, Chicago, 1964
Strauss, L., *The Argument and the Action of Plato's Laws*, midway reprint, Chicago, 1977.
Strauss, L., *Studies in Platonic Political Philosophy*, with an introduction by Thomas L. Pangle, Chicago, 1983

Taylor, A., *Plato, the Man and his Work*, London, 1948
Taylor, A., *The Laws of Plato*, London, 1934

Vernant, J-P., *Mythe et pensée chez les Grecs*, Paris, 1971, two vols
Vlastos, G., *Socrates*
Vlastos, G., 'Review of Morrow' (I 939), *PhR*, 50 (1941), pp. 50, 93–95
Vlastos, G., 'Equality and Justice in Early Greek Cosmologies', *CP*, 42 (1947), pp. 156 ff
Voegelin, E., *Plato*, Louisiana, 1966

Webster, T.B.L., *The Tragedies of Euripides*, London, 1967
Wilamowitz, V., *Platon*, Berlin, 1919, vol. I
Wilamowitz, U.V., *Platon und Werke*, Berlin, 1929
West, M., *Hesiod, Works and Days*, Oxford, 1978
Woozley, A.D., 'Plato on Killing in Anger', *PQ*, (1972)
Woozley, A.D., 'Socrates on Disobeying the Law' in G. Vlastos, *Socrates*, pp.221–318

Zeller, E., *Plato and the Older Academy*, London, 1876

Classical Texts and Translations

I have found T. Saunders' translation of the *Laws* both readable and faithful to the Greek text, unlike others that lack one of the two qualities mentioned above. His bibliography on the *Laws* with his additional citations to 1975 has also been particularly helpful to me.

The Greek text of all the works of Aristophanes, Aeschylus, Sophocles and Euripides is included in the Oxford Classical Texts series, published by the Oxford University Press. Translations of all the comedies and tragedies quoted in my thesis are from the Penguin Classics. Most of the works of Homer, Hesiod, Thucydides, Herodotus, Plutarch, Xenophon, Aristotle and the dialogues of Plato are from the Penguin Classics except where otherwise specified. The Greek texts of Plato's works are taken from the series of Oxford Classical Texts.

The fragments cited in my book are taken from the *Tragicorum Graecorum Fragmenta*, edited by A. Nauck (2nd edn., Leipzig, 1839; revised with supplement by B. Snell, Hildesheim, 1964).

Aeschylus, the *Oresteia (Agamemnon, Choephori, Eumenides)*
Aeschylus, *Seven Against Thebes*
Aristophanes, *Clouds*
Aristophanes, *Ecclesiazusae*
Aristophanes, *Frogs*
Aristophanes, *Lysistrata*
Aristophanes, *Wasps*
Aristotle, *The Athenian Constitution*
Aristotle, *Eudemian Ethics*
Aristotle, *Metaphysics*
Aristotle, *Nicomachean Ethics*
Aristotle, *On the Heavens*
Aristotle, *Physics*
Aristotle, *Politics*
Aristotle, *Rhetoric*

Athenaeus, *Deipnosophists*
St Augustine, *De Civitate Dei*
Cicero, *De Legibus*
Cicero, *De Oratore*
Diodorus, *Thespies*
Euripides, *Hecuba*
Euripides, *Medea*
Euripides, *The Trojan Women*
Herodotus, *The Histories*
Hesiod, *Theogony*
Hesiod, *Works and Days*
Homer, *The Iliad*
Homer, *The Odyssey*
Diogenes Laertius, *Lives of the Philosophers*
Plato, *The Apology*
Plato, *Crito*
Plato, *Epistle* VII
Plato, *Euthydemus*
Plato, *Euthyphro*
Plato, *Gorgias*
Plato, *The Laws*
Plato, *Lysis*
Plato, *Minos*
Plato, *Parmenides*
Plato, *Phaedo*
Plato, *Phaedrus*
Plato, *Politicus*
Plato, *Protagoras*
Plato, *The Republic*
Plato, *The Sophist*
Plato, *Symposium*
Plato, *Theaetetus*
Plato, *Timeaus*
Plutarch, *On Sparta*
Plutarch, *Theseus*
Sappho, *Poems and Fragments*, translated by Josephine Balmer, 1984
Sophocles, *Ajax*
Sophocles, *Antigone*
Sophocles, *Oedipus at Colonus*

Sophocles, *Oedipus the King*
Theognis, *Elegies*
Theophrastus, *Characters*
Thucydides, *The Peloponnesian War*
Xenophon, *Memorabilia* (Memories of Socrates)
Xenophon, *Oeconomicus*

List of Periodicals

ACI	*Atti del Convegno Internazionale sul tema: delta tribù allo stato*, Roma
APA	*American Philology Association*
BICS	*Bulletin of the Institute of Classical Studies of the University of London*, London, 31–34 Gordon Square
BSA	*The Annual of the British School of Archaeology at Athens*, London
CJ	*Classical Journal*
CP	*Classical Philology*
CPh	*Classical Philology*, Chicago, University of Chicago Press
CQ	*Classical Quarterly*
CR	*Classical Review*
GRBS	*Greek, Roman and Byzantine Studies*, Durham NC, Dake University
Historia	*Revue d'histoire ancienne*, Wiesbaden, Steiner
Inst Cl	*Institute of Classical Studies*
JAA	*Journal of American Archaeology*
JHS	*Journal of Hellenic Studies*, London 33–34 Gordon Square
PhR	*Philosophical Review*
PQ	*Philosophical Quarterly*